Mar-Tech

a marriage made on earth

AMIT TIWARI

INDIA · SINGAPORE · MALAYSIA

ISBN 979-8-89066-873-8

I want to dedicate this book to to my mother **(Late Smt K. L. Tiwari)** and father **(Late Dr. G. S. Tiwari)** who planted the seed of knowledge in my mind and nurtured it. Who never stopped believing in me and always reminded me that words have the power to change the world. They gave me the gift of dreams and the ability to realize them.

To my wife **Sonal** my partner, my best friend, my greatest supporter. She has walked every step of this journey with me. Who has been my most profound inspiration and always pushes me to reach for the stars.

To my elder son **Archit** the light of my life, who is my heart living outside of my body.

To my younger son **Aarush** who fills my heart with joy each and every day. Who continues to inspire me to tell stories that matter.

I want to express my sincere gratitude to all my family, friends and well-wishers for their kind support and guidance.

Gururbrahma gururvishnuh, gururdevo maheshwarah |
Guruhsakshat parabrahma, tasmai shrigurave namah ||

Contents

Reviews

In an increasingly digital world, the importance of effective marketing tech cannot be overstated. Amit Tiwari's book, "Martech: A Marriage Made on Earth" cleverly uses an analogy based on relationships and how they need to be nurtured with collaboration, compromise, and understanding, to talk about how to build successful Marketing and Technology partnerships. This book is a must read for every brand marketer or entrepreneur looking to unlock growth and build successful businesses.

– Sarita Digumarti

Co-Founder and COO, Jigsaw Academy

In his book "Martech: A Marriage Made on Earth" Amit explores the intimate relationship between Marketing and Technology in an interesting and relatable manner. There are several concepts that he lays out in a lucid manner including Total Marteching. The use of case studies and brand stories makes it a valuable and pragmatic guidebook for all Marketers.

– Rajesh Ramakrishnan

Managing Director, Perfetti van Melle India Pvt Ltd

Practitioners have a vantage point that professors and theorists do not have. Amit Tiwari has that advantage of being a CMO and having been a user of mar-tech to be able to know what is impactful and what is not. Amit having used mar-tech tools knows how to separate the grain from the chaff. Marketing and Technology is a marriage made in heaven for leaders, entrepreneurs, CMOs and Brand Managers who wish to grow their brands and businesses through deployment of Martech. 14 chapters are like making the marriage double strong as it involves 7 fears two times or be it the 7-year itch twice. (Kidding.) Amit's book is a practitioner's guide to mar-tech and a must read for all investors in mar-tech.

– Dr. Annurag Batra

Chairman *BW Businessworld* and founder *exchange4media,*
Angel investor, Author and TV Show host

Amit Tiwari's new book is a thoughtful, timely and highly engaging exploration of the converging worlds of Marketing and Technology. The book's use of marriage as a vehicle to describe the complex relationship between these two disciplines is as insightful as it is original. Part history book, part crystal ball "Martech: A Marriage Made on Earth" will prove an invaluable resource for senior professionals and new graduates alike.

– Tim Howat

Managing Director, APAC - TIME

The debut publication by Amit Tiwari, entitled "Martech: A Marriage Made on Earth", effectively illustrates the correlation between marketing and technology through the captivating analogy of a relationship.

Several concepts and frameworks are used to clearly define the complex role both marketing and technology must undertake. The future does not solely revolve around the domains of marketing or technology. The amalgamation of these two entities will have a profound impact on shaping the future. Martech refers to the technological processes and tools employed in the conversion of unprocessed data into meaningful insights, hence empowering marketers to make well-informed and strategic choices. The convergence of marketing and technology has facilitated a multitude of opportunities, fundamentally transforming the manner in which brands establish connections, engage, and cultivate relationships with their target audiences. Amit's book provides a comprehensive analysis of the various dimensions of this synergy and its significance in the field of marketing.

Marteching can be likened to a symphony, wherein technology orchestrates the flawless flow of communication and captivates clients at each interaction point. Amit's book is expected to provide significant assistance to aspiring marketing professionals, serving as a beneficial guidebook for both experienced practitioners and entrepreneurial individuals.

– Sanjay Gupta

Country Head and Vice President, Google India

Author Bio

Amit Tiwari is a strategic marketing technology leader with a global influence and a knack for changing the game as soon as he's on the field. While many may laudably speak of reaping the synergies between Marketing, Technology, Media Planning, Data Science, Integrated Communication and Talent Management, intrapreneurial Amit has been busy applying them within large organisations such as ***Philips*** and ***Havells***, with unstinting success. His new-age marketing approach has withstood the test of time and earned the appreciation of his peers (and of leading business journals, for whom he now writes regular columns). He is currently serving as the Global Head of the Marketing Demand Center at ***Tata Consultancy Services***. Be it leadership development or business development, database management or channel management, there are a few things the ***ISB***, ***Kellogg*** and ***Wharton*** educated Tiwari hasn't done, and done splendidly. Nevertheless, there is always a first time for everything, and the book in your hand is a first even for Amit. We hope it makes a good enough first impression for you to come back for seconds.

Foreword

Presenting the familiar in an unfamiliar fashion is a great communication device. Amit's book does the same in a very readable, educative and informational way.

In fact, audiences for any book have several audiences. There are experts who read, to stay in touch with a changing world (like good doctors). In this case, young marketers, students and curious common readers who find marketing and tech a marriage of a familiar with a seemingly unfamiliar.

Pleasantly, Amit's book will be educational and enjoyable for all. I believe that everyone need not be a musical instrument player, but it helps if you are into music appreciation. It helps to respect what you may not be an expert at. Having been to both—first at ***Havells*** and now at ***TCS***—shows that the author is a martech professional and also an appreciator of both the areas.

Look at the example of great innovators like ***Apple, Nike,*** various cars and more, you will find great tech-based products also have great Marketing history. If you believe this, then perhaps one day somebody will write a story about your story.

I wish this book and Amit great success in impacting minds in this new world, where a lot is changing very fast in technology, marketing and of course, marriages.

– Piyush Pandey

Chairman of Global Creative &
Executive Chairman, Ogilvy India

Preface

Why did I write this book?

Am I, Amit Tiwari, an author? No more than a town crier is a poet. But, like the town crier, I do believe I bear a timely message which is in the interest of the hearer. If you will pardon the manner in which the message tumbles out, and take it to heart, I believe my job will be done. For, my message carries with it the weight of experience and a sense of urgency. You see, in my 25 years as a marketer I've often seen tools get the better of people. This applies to tools new and old, but especially to the new and unfamiliar. The lack of understanding the WHY behind the tool leads to mishaps in HOW that tool is handled and mastered.

Take for instance, digital media. To an Enterprise mind, this tool can do so much: increase efficiency, standardise expectations, enhance an experience. To a Marketing mind, the same attributes would translate to: increasing *media* efficiencies, standardising *channel/trade* expectations, and enhancing an *advertising* experience. On the stray occasion where Marketing wanders into a less defined territory–such as designing a *product* experience–it nevertheless confines itself to its discipline.

Therein lies the challenge, and the opportunity. Can we reintroduce Marketing and Technology, and have them date for a while, before walking Martech down the aisle? The book you are holding sets out to do just that.

Throughout this book, I refer to "we" rather than "I", which isn't an acknowledgment of the royal "we", but rather a hat tip to the many hearts and minds that have brought about this book, who would rather remain unnamed.

When we sat down to write, we first admitted the near-impossible task of putting out a book on a subject that would change manifold by the time of the book's release. We resolved this in two ways: first, we decided to base everything on fundamental marketing and human truths, which never change. And second, we decided to treat this project as if it were a book we had already published last year, and whose second edition we wished to bring out.

That meant first writing it, bringing it to perfection, and then rewriting the entire book as one, in a final sprint before going to press.

We hope you find it as enjoyable and enriching in the reading as we did in the writing.

Acknowledgment

How do I summarise 2-and-a-half decades of mentors, pioneers and leaders that I've been blessed to work with and learn from?

It is as futile as trying to make a bank statement from the wealth of wisdom I have received from them.

But when I asked myself "How do I acknowledge one, without acknowledging all," I realised I had my answer: I could acknowledge one, while acknowledging all. I decided to name them all "Dhanush", derived from a Sanskrit word that means both gratitude and wealth.

Now that that's sorted, let me tell you what I owe Dhanush. A credit report, if you will.

I owe Dhanush for introducing me to the discipline of Marketing, a field rich in insight and learning. I owe him for showing me the ropes in my first internship. I owe him for the many tea sessions he had with me, where he dropped pearls of practical wisdom which I gladly stooped to pick up. I owe him for my first promotion, and for the chat he had with me, which was worth more than any pay hike. I owe him for seeing that I was the right man for the impossible jobs, and that he could go home while I put the fires out for the night. I owe him for solving his toughest challenges by just sending me into the fray. I owe him for believing in me when even I wouldn't.

Then, after helping me master Marketing, he introduced me to Tech, for which I am ever grateful. I thank him for making that transition as eventful as it was frictionless. I thank him for never acknowledging me as a designation, but seeing in me a lifelong learner. I thank him for helping me tame the things that ever change, while mastering the ones that never do.

Thanks for everything, Dhanush. You know who each of you are.

Scan for digital version of the images in this book

PART I

INTRODUCTION

Chapter 1

"Marketing, Meet Tech; Tech, Meet Marketing"

Humans have always had an intimate relationship with their tools. They create tools to serve them, and the tools assist them as they tame the world.

To understand the relationship between Marketing and Technology, we must first understand human beings' relationship with either. We will introduce them in that order, and you will soon see why.

Let us first introduce

Marketing

Marketing serves commerce, which comprises markets. Since the earliest of times, humans have served their own interests by trading across markets, brokering exchange and growth for themselves and others.

In all this time, while markets have changed, marketing has not. How could it? Its fundamentals have driven commerce since the very beginning, honing the tried and true precepts we honour today.

Can any company, organisation or institution cease to be a marketer? Yes, when they cease to be about people. One can sooner rid oneself of the "Finance" division, the "Procurement" team or even "Technology" than the discipline of Marketing.

"How?" You may ask. This may even sound preposterous to some: "Is the author suffering from a bout of self-importance, placing his own discipline above the others?" We're glad the question comes about, for the answer is instructive. Think for a moment about any division in an enterprise. Let's say "Sales".

Can a sale take place without someone being marketed to? No, for the buyer must first be aware of the product or service being sold, before deciding to buy. That's Marketing. Let us take "Finance". Surely, one would think, no company could exist without cash flow. And one would be right. No company could, because credit and funding only take you so far. But look closer: what occupies the Finance department? Transactions. What brought about those transactions? Marketing. You see, Marketing is the very lifeblood of an organisation. Everything else: Sales, Finance, Manufacturing, R&D, is an effect of which Marketing is the cause.

We will return later to build on this definition. But now we have a second introduction to make.

★ ★ ★

Enter

Technology

Looking smooth, suave, self-confident and self-assured. That's Technology. Always full of surprises. The life of the party. Wanna know where to get the best earbuds? Ask Technology. What comes after earbuds? Check with Technology. Is sound projection superior to bone conduction? We know who will know: Technology.

Technology is smart but not smug.

And that is why it is hard to find someone who does not like Technology. How could you hate something that does nothing in its own self-interest? Everything Tech does, it does to improve life around it. The field of medicine? Healthtech makes it better. Education? Edtech's teaching us a thing or two. Finance? Fintech for the win.

And in each of those examples, you see how Tech sees itself: not as leader, but enabler, suffixing itself to the many disciplines it improves.

As an exercise, try and see how many words you could prefix with "tech".

Affix "tech" to the below words as you find appropriate		
PREFIX		SUFFIX
______	**Ad**	______
______	**Agri**	______
______	**Bio**	______
______	**Edu**	______
______	**Fin**	______
______	**Health**	______
______	**Insur**	______
______	**Med**	______

None, right? It's no different with Marketing. Just the way it appends itself after "agri" or "bio" or "ad", Technology appends itself to Marketing to form Martech. And that's the perfect segue to introduce the two to each other.

★ ★ ★

Well before you make the introduction you notice that Marketing and Technology are no strangers to each other.

Their paths have crossed, and they've emerged better for it.

You think back to the first wagon hitched to a donkey that carted one's wares to the market. And to the first crude weighing scale, with which to mete out fair measure. And to the counting pebbles, that helped compute one's net income at the close of the day.

But now the time has come to make that introduction, and you make it. You watch the two survey each other, filing away important information that will come up later.

They smile and nod, and talk for a while. From then on, you see them off and on, always together, enjoying each other's company. "I did a good thing", you reassure yourself.

And you did. You took the time to get to know them both, saw a terrific fit, and did not hesitate to make the introduction.

What could go wrong?

Can things go wrong? Of course, as in any relationship. And that is why this book doesn't end here.

Read on to know how Marketing and Technology can have a flourishing and fruitful relationship, and your role in keeping it that way.

~ ~ ~ ~

Chapter 2

Evolution of Technology & Marketing

What came first: Technology or Marketing?

At first this seems like a chicken and egg situation. But that is why we introduced the Marriage analogy, because it reminds us that Technology and Marketing are equals; one may precede the other, but needn't bring forth the other.

That said, purely by logic, we can surmise that Tech came before Marketing. For, as we established in the previous chapter, "tech" is nothing but "tool", and humans have always crafted tools to master their environment.

Consider for a moment a farmer in prehistoric times, wielding a yoke for subsistence long before yielding a surplus. Only when the plough reaps more than his fair share, will he then see the need for a cart to take it to market. Truly a case of the horse coming before the cart (as it ought).

When we look at the evolution of Technology and Marketing we see not only that Technology came first, but that it assisted Marketing in its emergence, and is critical even now in Marketing's survival and growth.

Evolution of Technology			Evolution of Marketing
Technology comes from the Greek 'techne', meaning art and craft, and 'logos', meaning word and speech.			*Marketing comes from the Latin 'mercatus', meaning to trade.*
Potter's Wheel is invented	5000 BC	4000 BC	Wheeled vehicle invented
Babylonians leverage architectural tools to build zoned cities	4000 BC	3000 BC	Zoning policies confine trading to particular parts of cities
Coinage introduced to pay mercenaries of war	600 BC	300 BC	Coinage introduced to facilitate merchants in trade
Greek agora and Roman forum formed for sale of goods	500 BC	200 BC	Markets begin to cluster based on goods sold
Chinese invent papermaking	200 BC	700 AD	Chinese begin using paper banknotes
Introduction of the cannon in land warfare	1400 AD	1600 AD	Integration of the cannon on sea to protect trade interests
Trade limited to land, and short inland river routes	pre 1300 AD	post 1300 AD	Trade moves across oceas with invention of compass
First commercial steam-powered device introduced	1700 AD	1900 AD	Compound steam engine leads to increased international trade

Today Technology has rendered marketplaces online i.e., accessible from anywhere, and the rest as they say, is history.

Although we've only seen a few, there've been endless examples of Technology serving Marketing over the centuries. You see, Technology exists to serve.

Beyond its immediate service towards human subsistence, Technology has always facilitated trade, of which markets are but one kind:

- health (healthtech)
- agriculture (agritech)
- education (edutech)

and other human trades, always suffixing itself AFTER the trade, as we saw in the previous chapter.

In turn, Marketing serves Technology by increasing its reach and purpose. It takes it out of the home and into the market, exposing it to more humans and human applications. In a sense, Tech is Marketing's first and most valued customer. You see, Marketing exists to offer and transfer value.

So, we gathered that Technology exists to serve, and Marketing exists to offer and transfer value. And there, early into this book, we have a proto-definition of Martech: the ever-evolving service of value offering and transfer.

Now, we look for examples of their convergence.

Since Technology serves Marketing, it is no surprise to see antiquity peppered with examples of their convergence.

Let us take a small excursion through a Middle Eastern market from over 20 centuries ago, and see what we find.

It is the wee hours of the morning, shortly after daybreak, and a peasant trundling along in an oxcart reaches sight of the marketplace. His joke that "Haichu will surely return empty-handed this time" was not received well by his wife, and he chortled to himself as he recalled it. He caught sight of the weather vane, which told him the wind was blowing West. "A good omen", Haichu assured himself. He halted the cart, tethered his ox, and began to offload his produce.

How many trade-facilitating tools do you see yet? We see two: the oxcart and the weather vane. But observe what Haichu does next.

He lowers a back flap, and sends his crates sliding down.

There we have an example of the inclined plane, one of humankind's earliest technologies.

His ox snorts, reminding him not to forget to leave out the feeding trough and pail like he did last time.

Don't worry about those tools, they have nothing to do with the trade of today.

Let us follow Haichu the peasant as he hoists the crates and begins to carry them down the covered walkway to his stall, which, to his delight, is covered in a bright red cloth. My pomegranates will sell out, he thinks, grinning. He sets down the last of the crates, and instals a crude wooden board displaying the price of his wares. The market begins to stir. A lettuce farmer in the nearby stall makes his first sale. The customer peers closely at the goods in the weighing scale, and at the weights, in response to which the farmer promptly adds another lettuce that tilts the scales over. The happy customer now catches sight of a stall with very bright red pomegranates, and a beaming peasant offering him one. He sees the price displayed on a wooden board, and approaches. Moments later Haichu has sold his first crate, and soon after, every last one. Later that day the farmers and other merchants at the marketplace sit down to count their coins. They sit there counting awhile, since the covered walkways did a lot to keep the harsh sun out, and the happy customers in.

Do you see what we see?

And what do we see? Martech: technology serving marketing. This example showed us 3 aspects of technology's facilitation of marketing: logistics, experience and transaction.

You will notice that centuries later, not much has changed.

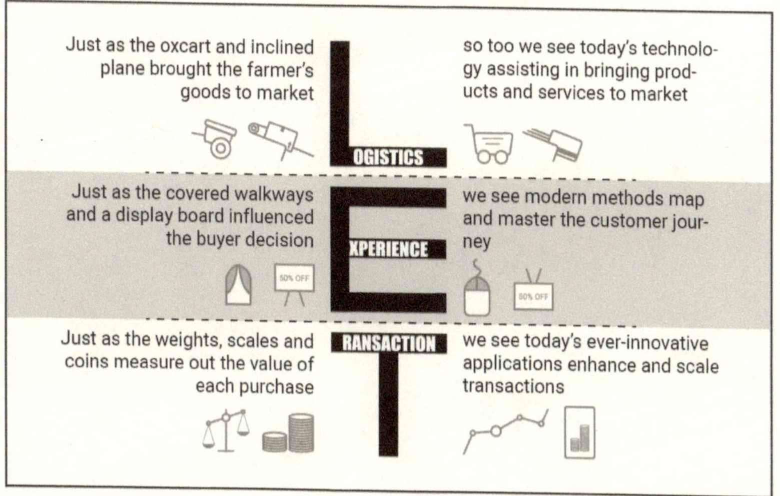

You know, there is one aspect of the medieval marketing experience that we left out. We reserved it for the end, because it is truly a marvellous example of early Martech at work. And here it is. Did you know that even as far back as 5000 years ago, markets began to be located at the town center? Well you may've known that, but here's the interesting bit: they soon came to be surrounded by alleyways where you would find artisans such as metal-workers, leather workers, potters and carpenters working on their wares, taking a break from their work only on market day. Don't you see the same today?

That is as enduring an example of Martech as you will find. And with that, we bring Part I to a close, and now turn to study the natural courtship between the two disciplines, beginning with their most magnetic attributes. As we will discover, opposites not only attract, but complement.

~ ~ ~ ~

PART II

COURTSHIP

Chapter 3

Opposites Attract

Notice how well compatible couples complement each other? One leads with heart, the other with head. One is more instinctive, the other more reflective. One is stimulated by action, the other by conversation.

We see the same compatibility take place when examining the positive attributes of Marketing and Technology. Let us first look at the attributes of both, before seeing them complement each other.

Positive Attributes of Marketing

Like Tech, Marketing too is innovative, always on, and in the service of people. But both go about it very differently. While Technology can and does cater to people's needs, Marketing is more naturally predisposed to it. As we read in the previous chapter, Marketing caters to the needs of others as soon as its own subsistence is seen to. It exists to trade, not hoard, thriving more on story than storage. **Marketing is people-oriented.**

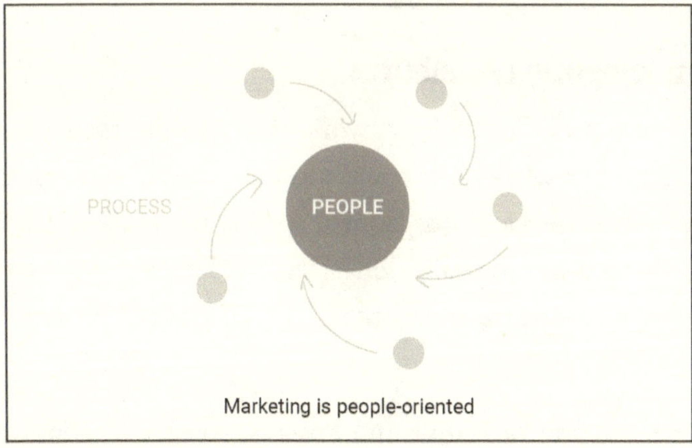

Marketing is people-oriented

Positive Attributes of Technology

While technology does serve people, that is not its primary orientation. Technology collects and catalogues information, observes patterns, connects dots and marks trends, which a more people-focused discipline could ill afford to do. As we read in the previous chapter, Technology caters to the discipline to which it is attached, bringing order, stability and predictability to the chaos. **Technology is process-oriented.**

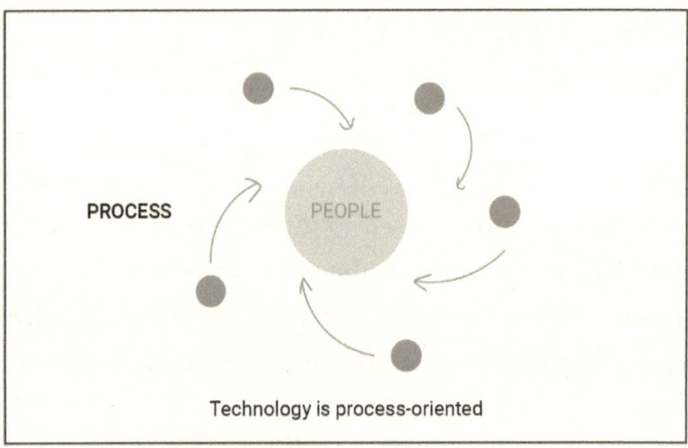

Technology is process-oriented

Complementing Attributes

Marketing and Technology work well within their silos of operation, but when they come together, magic happens. Costs are trimmed, propositions honed, spends repurposed, feedback implemented and overall, things look promising. It's 1+1=3[3]. The whole isn't just greater than the sum of its parts, but a multiple of it.

From the aspect of People and Process, you see the transfer of knowledge and opportunity between Marketing and Technology.

Marketing's People skills provide a new dimension to Process, and Technology's Process skills do vice versa.

However, there is a third aspect which sees an even greater symbiosis between Marketing and Technology, and that is called Practice.

The Practices of an organisation, division or team improve over time, and are an outcome of functions like Marketing and Technology performing at their best.

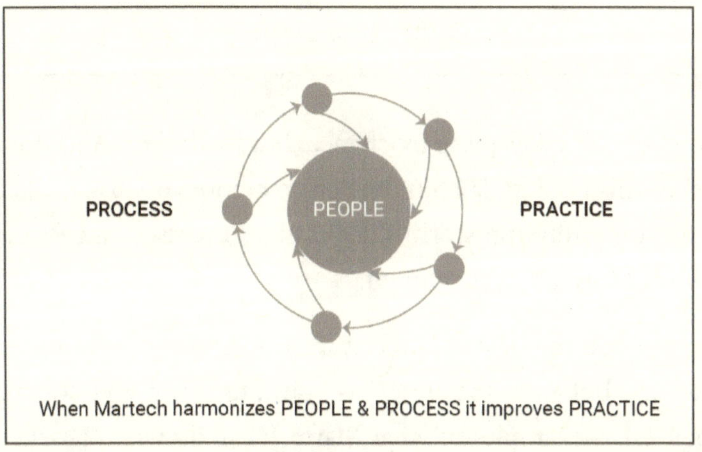

When Martech harmonizes PEOPLE & PROCESS it improves PRACTICE

Remember when we termed Martech *"the ever-evolving service of value offering and transfer"*? Here's where that proto-definition begins to get hands and legs. With Technology and Marketing functions operating at their optimum, several possibilities are laid open. First, the silos start to work in sync. If you've never seen that happen, you want to. Then, team leads talk, understand each other, and next thing you know, cross-functional teams are working in unison and earnest towards common goals.

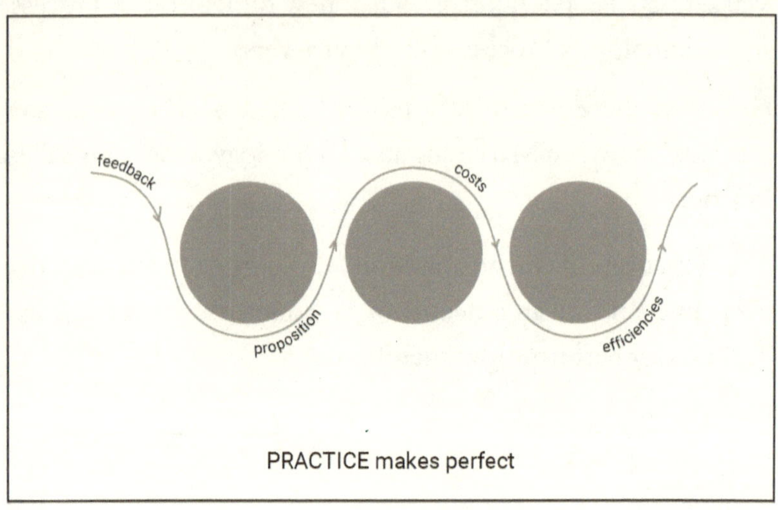

PRACTICE makes perfect

None of this takes place by chance, but by design. And it is the goal of this book to lay out the design before you, to enable you to meaningfully transform the People, Processes and Practices in your Martech environment.

You will see the design laid out in simple terms in subsequent chapters, but now the time has come to show you concrete–albeit early–examples of what Martech can do when Marketing and Technology come together with purpose.

We present before you 3 case studies featuring the complementary aspect of Marketing and Tech attributes in solving business problems.

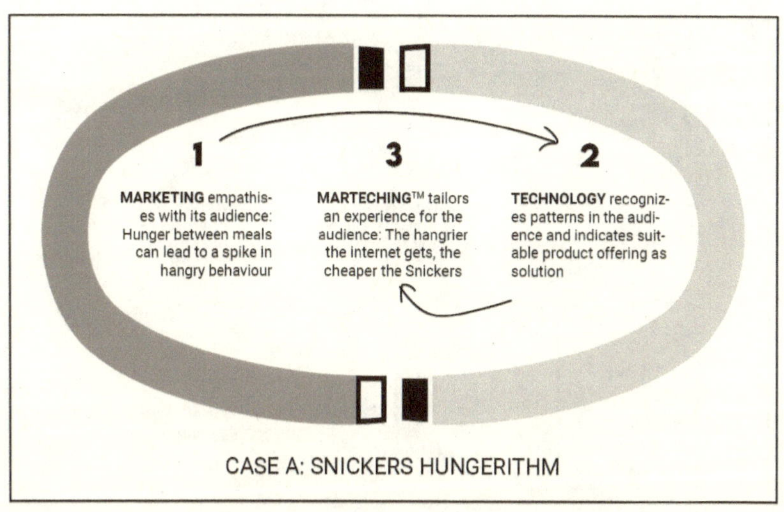

CASE A: SNICKERS HUNGERITHM

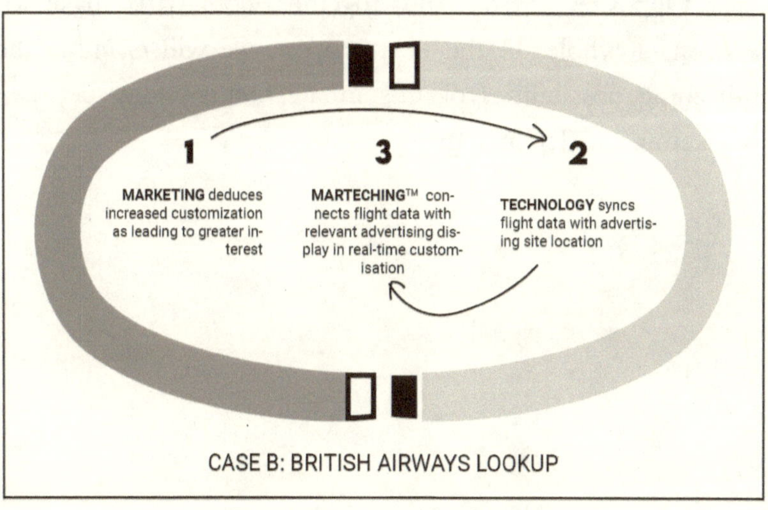

CASE B: BRITISH AIRWAYS LOOKUP

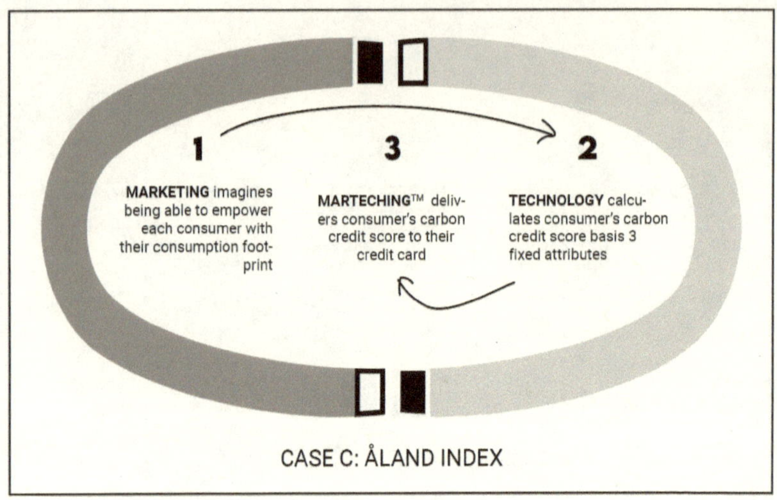

CASE C: ÅLAND INDEX

See? Opposites attract. And, together, both parts make for a stronger whole. In the next chapter, we will examine the intriguing possibilities of this innate compatibility between Marketing and Technology.

~ ~ ~ ~

Chapter 4

A Relationship of Compatibles

Marketing and Tech may be opposites, but they come together as composites. Of course they each have their respective roles and responsibilities, but as with any healthy marriage, both parties come together to function as one.

Hence, composite.

And just the way composites are hard to disassemble once they come together, it is hard to separate Marketing from Technology once they merge as Marteching™. Which is why it's best to get one's bearings before the genie's out of the bottle.

Hence, the book you are holding in your hand.

But all things considered, the word "composite" doesn't fully explain the phenomenon of Marteching™ done right. For that, we must turn to the word "alloy".

The Marteching™ Alloy

What is an alloy? The admixture of multiple elements coming together to create a newer and stronger entity.

It so happens that the traditional process of alloying offers us several lessons in getting our Marteching™ right. (Imagine that!)

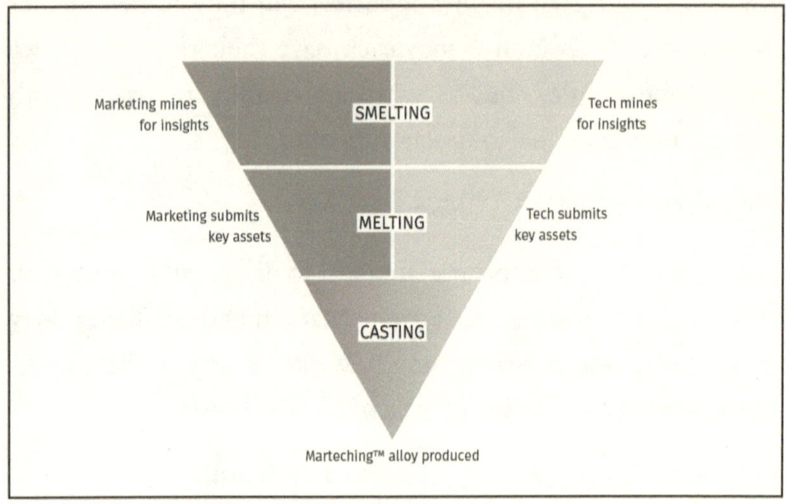

It all starts with **Smelting**, which is the process by which one extracts the vital metal from the ore.

Think about the Marketing process. You're in a boardroom, or out on the street, and you're extracting. Extracting information: "What does our audience expect of this solution?" Extracting meaning: "What does this behavioural insight tell us about possible need states?"

Now, do the same in a Technology environment. Once again you're in the boardroom, this time everyone's staring at the screen. The GANTT chart flashed temporarily, and now everyone's scrutinising last week's user analysis. You extract information: "Why is our beta rollout receiving so many false positives?" You extract meaning: "Could these new indicators actually point to untapped use cases that could be lucrative?"

Irrespective of where you stand in the great circular relay race involving Marketing and Tech, you're now ready for the next stage: introducing multiple elements together in the **Melting** process. So you take these elements, and to everyone's surprise, they begin to gravitate to one another, and then amalgamate. Marketing's "What does our audience expect" finds resonance in Tech's "our beta rollout is receiving false positives". Tech's "untapped use cases" answers Marketing's "behavioural insight".

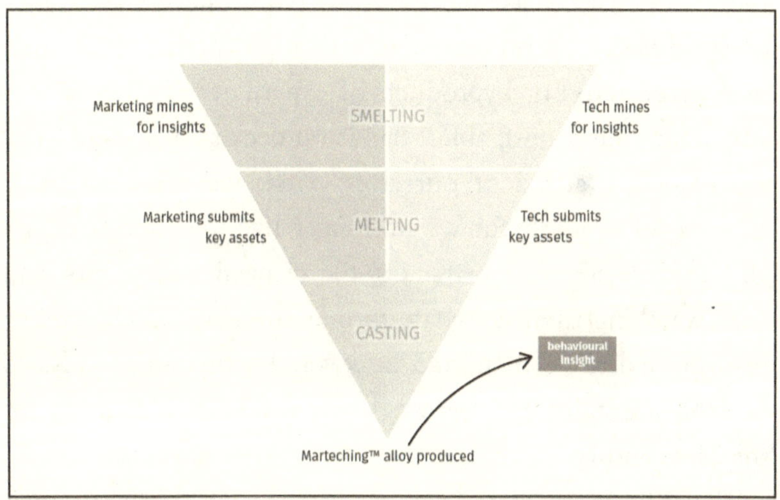

And right here, dear Martecher, we ask you to pause. Magic is about to happen. Those with zero foundrying experience will founder everything, so take the pause. And now, ask yourself: "Okay, where do we go from here?" "How must we meet this customer requirement?" "Who calls the shots?"

See? The answers don't come easy, and when they do, taking them is even less easy. Hence the pause. Take a breath, and then look closer, and you will be rewarded for it. Because what you're dealing with is no longer limited to your domain. KRAs clash. KPIs merge, and distort the signal. So before egos clash and the picture gets further distorted, you need to step back, and appreciate the fact that this is now unchartered territory. One slip and all is lost. It's happened to the best of us. Just compare the Global Fortunes this year, and 10 years ago, and you'll see only the temperate have survived.

So, stay tempered, as we watch our conveyor belt creak forward to the next stage: **Casting**. Here one requires every last ounce of steadiness and precision. (Neither are products of their own invention, but byproducts of experience. Which is why you want your sanest, ablest hands on deck at this stage.) But we're getting ahead of ourselves. First, we must assemble an array of moulds, for we no longer live in a one-size-fits-all world. Remember extracting the respective elements, and later watching them gravitate to one another? Surely, you've introspected since then, and discovered a myriad of ways to cast those insights and learnings into newer moulds made for the 21st century.

Now, with the moulds all lined up and ready, you may pour. Pour in all that hard work and determination. Pour in all those late nights where things went seemingly nowhere. Pour in every ounce of sweat and tears, which nobody thought mattered, and watch it all come together.

Of course, things don't come together by themselves ("ex nihilo nihil est", as the philosopher would say–"nothing comes from nothing"), and they didn't. Two seemingly disparate functions–Marketing and Technology–which sit cubicles, and even continents, apart, made the magic happen. And, it was all in a day's work. Cell C6 in a spreadsheet connected with bullet 17 in a SCRUM meeting, item #12 from the minutes connected with point 1 in the kickoff agenda, and voila, you have something special on your hands.

But that's only half the job done. The other half is repeating it profitably. At scale.

But you've got this. If it can be done once, it can, in theory, be done again. And again, and again. The trick is in "People" mastering "Process", until it becomes "Practice."

You see, the foundry you operated today is called P-P-P, and its design is the creative and collaborative triangulation of People, Process and Practice.

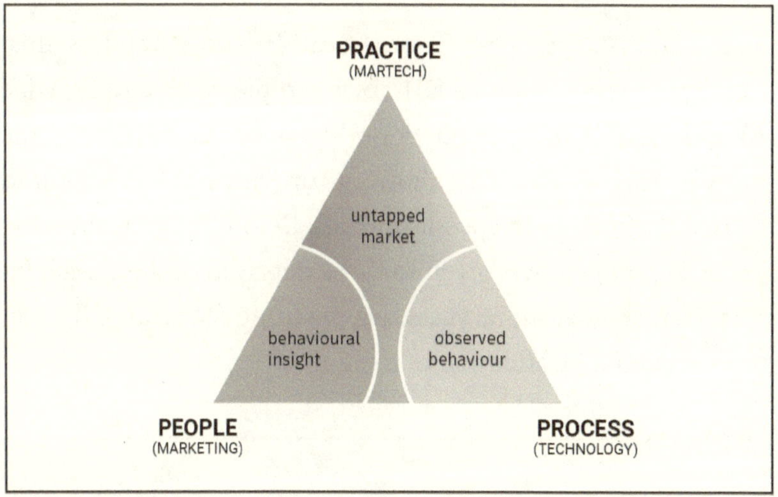

And when the three come together spectacularly, the only way forward is up.

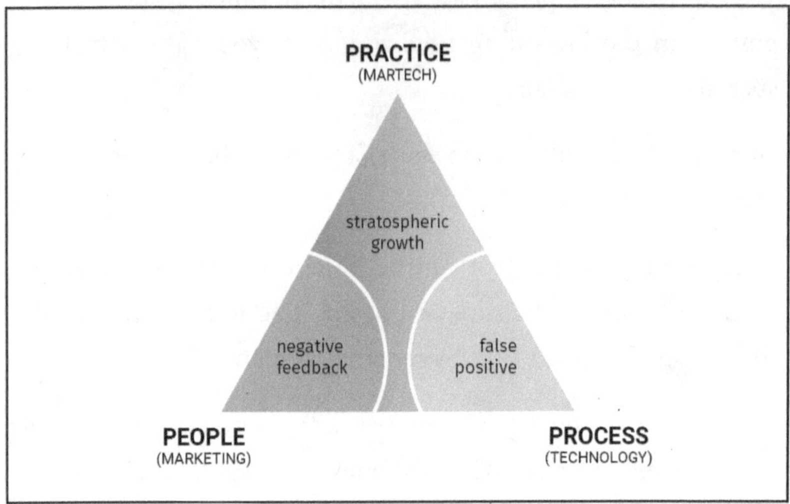

When that happens, the effect is something to behold.

Take for instance, *The Times*, Great Britain's quintessential masthead, who combined 831 voice samples with cutting-edge AI and months of laborious sound engineering to recreate the voice of John F. Kennedy, allowing America's 35th President to deliver his final speech posthumously. Before the global release, a special premiere was given to those deprived of the speech on that fateful day, albeit 55 years late, ensuring the echo of the pen reverberated long after that of the gun.

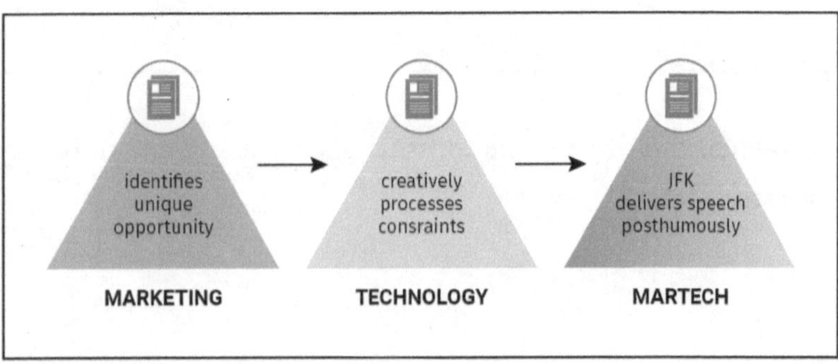

Next, a rather dated idea, but one that's yet to be bested: *Honda Civic*'s "The Other Side", a two-sided parallel storyline presented via a racy film, giving the viewer control over the experience with the 'R' key on the keyboard. The two drives were literally as different as day from night, offering the viewer a chance to test the "Racing" feature of the new Civic.

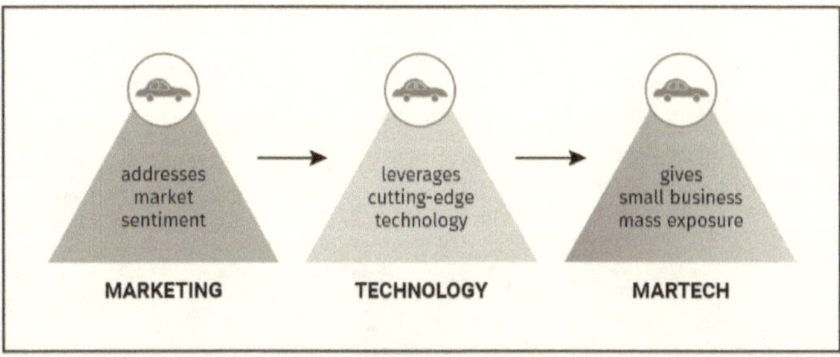

And finally, "Not Just a Cadbury Ad", which featured every conceivable retail outlet in India in a mass media television campaign during Diwali, giving small businesses a bigger boost than any marketer, techie or they themselves could ever imagine.

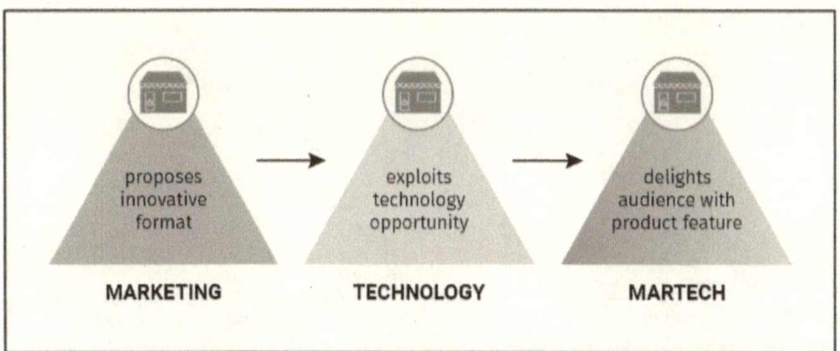

Now that's what Martech can do. If this has you excited, wait till you reach the next chapter. Go on, that page won't turn itself.

~ ~ ~ ~

Chapter 5

The Role of Creativity in the Relationship

As Marketing and Tech get to know each other, they one day discover: "We are both creative."

Indeed they are. How could they not be? Creativity spawned both markets and technology.

You see, it was creativity that said "He has salt, you have furs. Exchange." And, it was creativity that said "Let's create the horseless carriage" instead of "Let's get a faster horse".

The same creativity that gave us the wheel and the drainage system today drives technology. And Martech sits at the center of all the action.

One would love to have said Martech sits at the center *directing* the action, but that not being the case is what prompted this book in the first place.

So how CAN Martech direct the action? This chapter sets out to explain.

First, marketing revolves around People. No people, no markets, and no marketing. The same is the case with technology, which has no purpose apart from enriching human life.

This compels those in Martech to put empathy at the centre of their offering. Without empathy, people cease to find their interests mirrored, and move their value elsewhere.

Second, marketing is about Process. If marketing didn't offer solid science with all its empirical data and real-world results and analysis, it would've ceased as a core function a long time ago. And, in organisations and industries where marketing *has* ceased or stymied these operations, it *has* indeed rendered itself a support function, rather than the cog in the wheel.

This compels those in Martech to add a wholesome helping of evidence into their Martech mix.

Third, marketing is a Practice, and with tech enabling its most key practices–such as measurement, collaboration, forecasting and so on–Martech is all set to shed marketing of its inferiority complex as having proven to be one of the blunter tools in the toolbox.

This brings to Martech an expertise which has been hitherto wanting for the most part, in marketing.

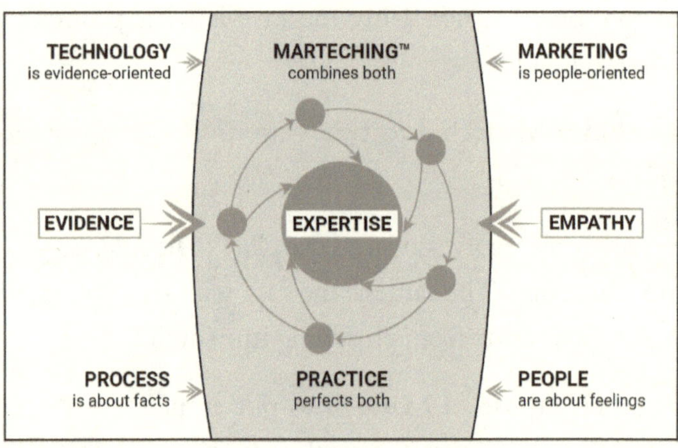

So you see, Martech's true strengths are in the compatibility of marketing and technology: Technology does for Marketing what Marketing could not do for itself, and in turn, Marketing helps Technology spread further asunder, establishing it as an inescapable part of the lives of billions. It is a relationship of mutual symbiosis.

But the key to unlocking this compatibility is creativity. Because, no relationship is free of challenges, and it is creativity that will help negotiate and negate them.

What makes it so? A 5-letter word that everybody hates: Change. Even those who thrive on it draw the line somewhere. And you will notice that Change affects human industry much like it does human relationships.

As always, the way out is for humans to face their fears, and collectively ACT; to anticipate, collaborate and transform challenges into opportunities.

Let's look at a few examples.

We'll begin with the Mill Blackbird, a revolutionary new car advertising technology (words we never expected to put together, but Martech surprises us every day) that is already driving heady results. If the folks at the Mill didn't anticipate the challenges on the road ahead for car advertisers, they wouldn't have collaborated with them to design the Blackbird, a solution that transforms how auto majors go to market. When confronted with change, Mill ACT-ed.

Let's look at H&M, a fast fashion label in a fast deteriorating world. They looked around themselves and saw the effects of the industry they were in, and decided to ACT: they anticipated the effects of waste on the planet, collaborated to introduce a waste-to-wear installation that turns old clothes into new right before your eyes in Stockholm, and are all ready to transform not just their operation, but the entire clothing industry.

And, let's not overlook a more everyday example, where Diesel connected the right dots between its product offering and the consumer experience, in taking their flexible jeans to market. They anticipated the trickiness of marketing a variant, collaborated with the right talent (a contortionist, imagine that!) to market it, and in doing so, transformed the way the industry markets itself online, with the Responsive Lookbook that riffs off the responsiveness of every conceivable browser environment.

If you wish to conquer challenges before they conquer you, you must ACT, too.

To know more about these and other interesting cases, you can visit www.themartechers.com.

~ ~ ~ ~

Chapter 6

Defining the Relationship

What is Marteching™?

Let's get straight to it. If Marteching™ is the fruitful marriage of Marketing and (customer-oriented) Technology, then it subsumes to itself all that makes these two functions tick.

Let's recall what makes Marketing tick:

- Anticipates and identifies customer needs
- Collaborates to introduce and improve its offering
- Repeat and loop

And what makes Tech tick?

- Helps anticipate and identify customer needs
- Collaborates to introduce and improve Marketing's offering
- Imitate and automate

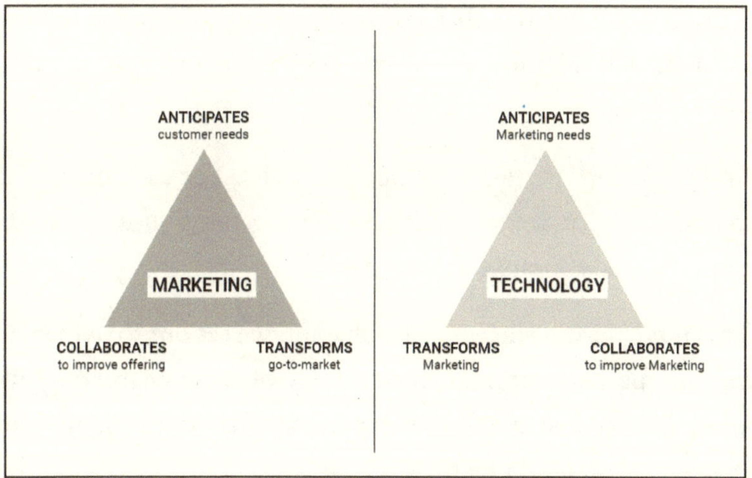

Perfect attributes, and perfect complementarity. It's almost begging for a merger.

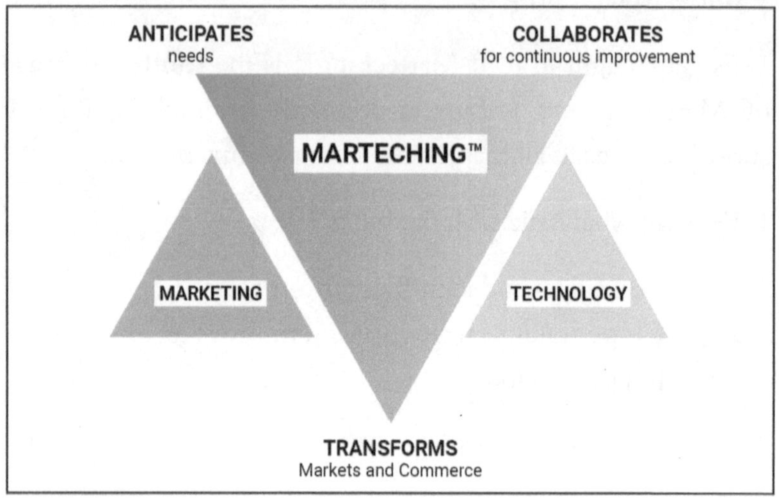

And there you have it—the perfect fusion of Marketing and Technology. Isn't it great to watch Marteching™ at work?

Now let's look at **Martech's Roles & Responsibilities**. Healthy relationships demand that the two parties make space for one another, and identify roles and responsibilities within those spaces.

And since both parties serve not themselves (or each other) but the customer, it is incumbent on the organisation to make the rules. Nobody wants a custody battle.

This is why, from the very first chapter, we set out to demarcate the unique and complementary roles of both Marketing and Tech. If you just recalled the prefix-suffix word game from chapter 1, you won't be the only one.

It's an intuitive reality: Tech enables Marketing to serve the customer. And that's Marteching™, in a nutshell. Remember the definition of Martech, from Chapter 2? Don't thumb back, we'll lay it out here, for you. We had called it: *"the ever-evolving service of value offering and transfer"*.

What's all this service in service of? The customer, of course. Take that out, and it's goodbye Marteching™. Remember that always: no customer, no Marketing. No Marketing, no Martech.

So you've seen the roles and responsibilities, now it's time to examine **Martech's Reality**. The consumer is changing. Back in the day, Ogilvy could've afforded to say "the consumer isn't a moron; she is your wife." Today, he might've been compelled to say "she is your daughter." Look around. More than the city, it's the citizen who never sleeps; the younger generation seem to be always on. And when they do sleep, they don't dream; they mine. Try swiping them for a library card–you won't find one. They simply whip out their phone and plough through reams of archived information: journals, dissertations, scholarly papers, case studies, you name it. They don't read books; they hear them. Yesterday information was at their fingertips; today it's on the tip of their lips, as they issue instructions to Siri, or whisper "goodnight Alexa". Growing up, we may've asked questions about the universe. The next generation is already asking questions about the metaverse.

This isn't the same generation you and I grew up in, and the sooner we realise that, the sooner we can serve them.

Going forward, we should equip Marketing and Tech for a world that's smarter, omnipresent and doesn't stop with satisfying its curiosity, but binges on it.

It is at this crossroads that larger questions ought to be asked, observations made, and hard decisions taken.

Addressing the New Realities

Let's navigate through a few questions that may be on your mind.

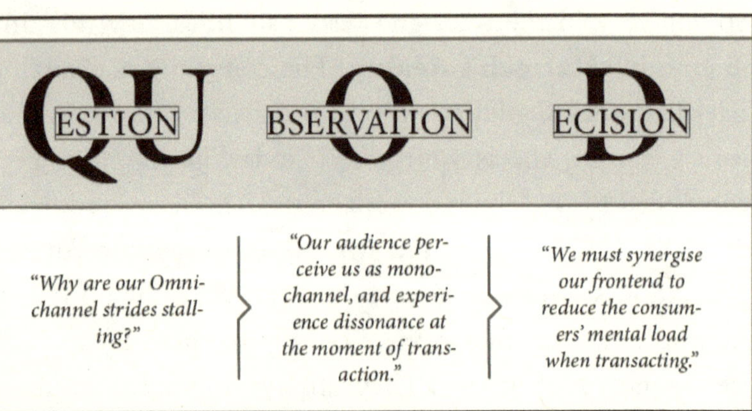

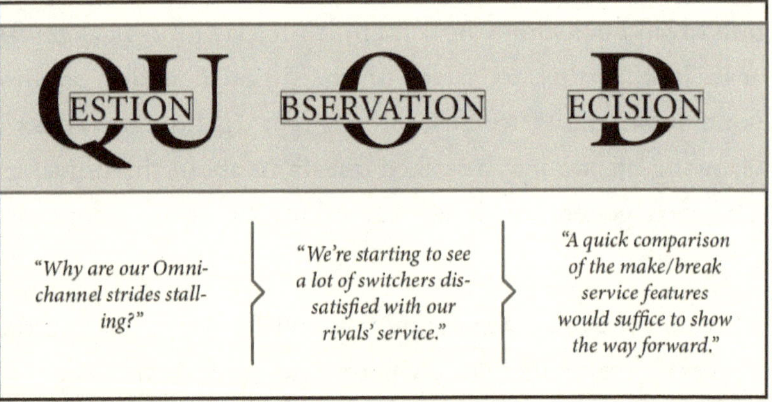

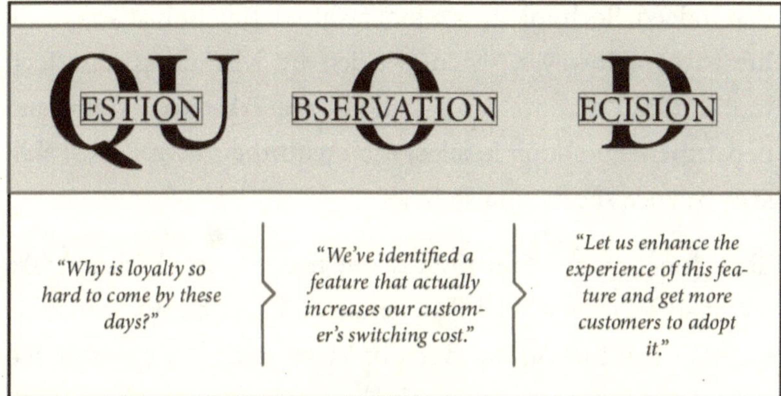

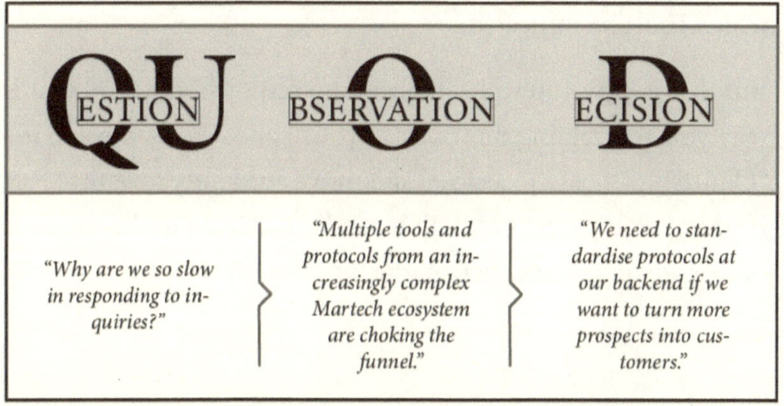

"QUOD?" is Latin for "What?" So now you have a handy acronym to apply, the next time you have a hard decision to make.

To summarise, Marteching™ is the fruitful coming together of Marketing and Technology in the interest of the consumer. While both Marketing and Technology are well aware of their respective roles and responsibilities, the convergence towards Marteching™ has led to a merging of the two, with a lot of grey area. When you take a step back from ground zero, you can see that indeed, Technology is a tool fashioned by humans to make life easier. However, when wielded by Marketing, the Tech tool can lead to more complications, exacerbated by teams and departments working in silos, each with their own KRAs, skill sets, balance sheets, and so on.

To dig oneself out of the morass, one needs to step back and take a high-level view of how Marketing and Technology can come together fruitfully in the avatar of Marteching™. As mentioned before, this convergence won't be easy to navigate, since both disciplines will bring their respective challenges to the fore, which must be mitigated.

But that is why you've been given the responsibility, and that is why you are holding this book in your hand. We now bring the "Courtship" phase to a close, and move stridently towards "Part III: Marriage", which we will begin by ushering in the minister of that alliance: the Chief Marteching™ Officer.

~ ~ ~ ~

PART III

MARRIAGE

Chapter 7

Meet the Chief Marteching™ Officer

And now, for that much awaited milestone: the marriage, where the twain shall meet and become as one.

Let us meet the minister of that happy union, the Chief Marteching™ Officer. What's her **role**? What **responsibilities** must she impress upon the 2 merging parties? Let us address these **roles** and **responsibilities** by first analysing the CMO as minister.

The CMO as minister

You cannot arbitrate over an area without first gaining expertise in it. And this is where all the years of experience gained in the marketing trenches come into play, giving the cross-functional and cross-domain martecher an edge over the rest.

When we think of the most successful CMOs of the day, we tend to think in terms of the most successful campaigns they've built, which may have genuinely led to their success, and that of the brands they were helming.

What doesn't often meet the eye is the successful teams they've built. You see, behind every successful CMO there stands a successful marketing team, and the reason CMOs with a winning streak have a winning streak is because they've grown used to leaving winning teams in their wake.

And this isn't easy in our era of increased complexity, where today's award-winning solution won't solve tomorrow's problem. The CMOs–being chiefs after all–oversee the tribe under their charge, stirred by a single imperative: grow or die. They're Cross-functional, Cross-domain, Eagle-eyed Hunters bushwhacking through the very Frontiers of Innovation, which makes for the appropriate acronym CHIEF, when rearranged.

Cross-function/domain

Turns out, Marketing isn't the only department that ought to put the customer at the centre. You know which other departments ought to? Every other.

That said, it often seems a pipe dream to get departments–even (or especially) the ones with "customer" in their name–to put the customer first. This is where the CMO's cross-functional and cross-domain experience comes in handy, because it helps if you have domain knowledge of the silos you hope to work around. And here, a caution for those keen on breaking down silos: you break only to rebuild. So, before taking the sledgehammer to a silo, familiarise yourself with its blueprint, because you may just have to reconstitute it all later.

Cross-function and cross-domain. What's the difference?

To investigate this difference, let us imagine a CMO, Rachel, tasked with integrating a cross-platform analytics solution whose success depends on all stakeholders contributing equally. Let's say, early on in her career, Rachel has worked, if only peripherally, with the customer service team. That's cross-functional experience. And let's say, 2 decades in, she's taken pains to complete an executive course on Big Data Analytics. That's cross-domain knowledge. Together, these 2 new facets give Rachel an edge over a lesser CMO.

1. Cross-function: Having teamed up with the customer service department during a business critical campaign in a previous role, Rachel experienced, if even intuitively, what drives and what ails that department.
2. Cross-domain: Having foreseen, acknowledged and then plugged a gap in her skill set, she successfully nixed the omnipresent "lost in translation" situation that so often occurs when departments conflate rather than collaborate.

What this tells us is that Marteching™ and marketing-adjacent departments can no longer work in silos. They may be discrete functions, yes, even requiring respectful distance between them, but they all share the same KRA. Organisations with siloed KRAs will see less fruitful collaboration between departments: a truly sobering reality, when confronted with the fact that only about 60 of the original Fortune 500 remain on the list today, and that the average tenure of companies on the S&P 500 has decreased from 33 years in 1964 to just 24 years today, and is expected to shrink to just 12 years by 2027*.

*McKinsey & Company

Life's too short to be dwelling on last year's wins and losses. You live, you learn, you commit the lessons to muscle memory, and you whack on.

Hunters

Were we kidding when we called CMOs hunters? I mean come on, is that just dressy language at work? One may be tempted to think so, but look closer. What does it take to be a successful hunter? Instinct, alertness, speed, stealth. Aren't these the very traits that make for success in marketing?

If they aren't, we'll tear out and eat this page right here. But, you can't help but admit, these are indeed the traits of both hunter and marketer. So what is the CMO hunting? Recognition? Fame? Those are byproducts. Hunkering down in the boardroom or clandestinely observing a trade in the street, what is the CMO in pursuit of? One thing, and one thing alone: enlisting a new customer. This may be among the most overlooked aspects of corporate life and even of marketing, but not to the marketer on the rise. Watching a prospect turn into a customer, however, is only half the job done. You've got to eke the lifetime value of that customer, for one, while turning that customer into a spokesperson for your brand. After all, what better media vehicle than a delighted customer?

Innovative

Now there's a buzzword we come across a dozen times before the lunch hour. But lest the word lose its zeal, let us quickly turn it to our purpose. What does innovation mean, and what marketer ISN'T innovative? Good questions.

This time, rather than turn to analogy, we will present actual innovations, each of which are backed by some of the world's most acknowledged CMOs. Caution, some of the below may cause a sharp intake of breath, and ejaculations of "Why didn't I think of that?" Ready? Let's begin.

Innovation #1: A real-time emotional insight tool developed to help the entertainment industry create, tweak and market content that will better resonate with their audience, now offering social media analytics.

Innovation #2: An audio fingerprinting technology that provides historical, real-time and predictive analysis of a brand's and its competitors' TV campaigns, enabling data-driven decision making and even forecasting potential outcomes, adjusting its own model for improved performance. (Pause to take a deep breath.)

Innovation #3: A sales compensation automation platform that allows companies to incentivise their sales teams with real-time payouts according to an approved commission structure, improving motivation and engagement.

Innovation #4: An AI-powered revenue attribution and forecasting platform using machine learning to build models that identify key touchpoints in a customer's journey and assign to each appropriate credit based on its impact on the customer's decision-making process. (No, we didn't make that up.)

Innovation #5: A B2B intent data provider that captures business intent by tracking the topics relevant to a client business and identifying (individuals within) companies researching those topics, helping client businesses further hone their account-based marketing strategies.

Who presides over these innovations? Chiefs. Chief Technology Officers, Chief Digital Officers, Chief Brand Officers, Chief Innovation Officers, Chief Customer Officers, Chief Solutions Officers (they exist) and Chief Marketing Officers, soon to be known world over as Chief Marteching™ Officers.

We could go on with the Marteching™ innovations, but maybe we'll reserve them for another time. Now, on to our next letter in the acronym soup, and it's anything but orthodox.

Eagle-Eyed

Ever seen an eagle perch in its natural habitat? Well, unless you climb the heady heights of a rocky crag, you likely wouldn't. But have you seen them swoop? You probably have.

The interesting thing about the eagle is it locks onto its prey miles before it has it in its claws. For, it is able to soar above it all, yet take in all the tiny details on the ground. And that is where the CMO is best placed: a few thousand feet above the air, taking it all in. Yes, we all love to see our leaders in the trenches, braving the elements like the rest of us. And for that we have the occasional swoop (an eagle's gotta eat and feed its own). But the place of the eagle-eyed CMO is high up in the air, eyes trained on the ground.

Because everybody talks of missing the forest for the trees, but miss out on this key detail: marketing is about people, and people are on the ground. It takes a birds-eye view to take in the forest, but an eagle-eyed view to take in both.

Frontiers

Imagine being asked to bushwhack away at "frontiers", when your home turf is on fire.

Much as it may feel that way in Marketing, that won't knock it off the to-do list. And so, alert the fire brigade and put out the fire. But don't put off that frontier so long that it becomes the next CMO's problem (even speeding up his arrival).

Gone are the days of continuous improvement. We're now living in an era of continuous innovation, the pace of which is so merciless, it doesn't just replace today's redundancy, but even yesterday's innovation. Thumb back to the innovation section. See those 5 innovations we called out? They will lose their lustre in less than a quarter, and before the year is up, will become staple fare.

Of course, patenting the non-obvious innovations will throw off the copycats, but they aren't the challenge: human ingenuity is. And, you're not the one to stand in the way of it.

If you're in Marketing, that's your job description. We innovate or else.

Being a CHIEF is a Chief Marteching™ Officer's **role**.

When it comes to **responsibilities**, you would expect a Chief Marteching™ Officer to be equal parts CMO and CTO. While the title will evolve over time, with some give and take between both (in the realm of Marketing), one can see ample opportunity for those with cross-domain and cross-functional knowledge and skills to integrate them under one killer title.

Duties of a CMO	Duties of a CTO/CIO
Champion Marketing	Champion Technology
Execute Marketing strategy by leveraging technology	Execute Tech strategy in the assistance of Marketing
Envision data-driven Marketing outcomes	Envision Marketing-driven data infrastructure
Design seamless customer experiences	Deliver seamless customer experiences
Collaborate across silos in driving business goals	

So, Big CHIEF. How do you go about being a Cross-functional, Cross-domain, Eagle-eyed Hunter bushwhacking your way through the very Frontiers of Innovation every or any day of the week? Let's face it, we CMOs are no spring chickens. With the better part of 2 decades, give or take, under (and over) our belt, do we really expect this of ourselves? Didn't Michael Porter ask us to keep entry barriers high? Why are we pushing back frontiers and breaking down silos now? What's changed? Are we really doing this?

Silly as these questions may sound out loud, you know at some point you've been thinking it. (*"Groan, another Marketing guru telling me how to do my job."*) The answers, as is so often the case, are to be found in yourself. You start by getting situational awareness, enough to know that you don't know enough. Once you admit that, you go in search of the knowledge you lack, of which there is no dearth in the era in which we live.

Let's start with situational awareness: admitting you don't know as much as you ought. How do you fix that? Simple. Read what everybody's reading. Read what nobody's reading. Ditto for the verbs "watch", "follow", "think" and "observe".

Next, knowledge. Nobody likes a know-it-all, but there's no harm being the one they seek when they want answers. Aim to be the first person people check with, and the last person people check with. At times, that knowledge is contained not on a server somewhere, but in a peer working alongside you. Oftentimes, that peer is you. Ask questions. Especially those no one else is asking. Look beyond easy answers. Look into the reams of research your organisation has already produced over the years. Spend time with the interns. Talk to someone in Sales. This is, after all, a people business. Lose touch, you lose the game.

That being said, staying informed is one thing, but turning information into innovation is quite another. And here you're all on your own, because just as "there's more ways to skin a cat", there's no single way to innovate, or to stay innovative. It helps to know what's out there, what's being done and by whom, and then, to have the sheer desire and will to look past it with the conviction that inside you could be the next breakthrough waiting to break through. (Why not?)

As challenging as all of this may sound, we've only discussed one facet of the CMO: the minister, arbitrating the marriage of Marketing and Technology. Strap yourself in, because things are about to get even more interesting.

The CMO as midwife

What is the ultimate purpose of marriage, if not to produce offspring? In coming together to produce its own, Marketing and Tech, like any couple, undergo the very same experiences as their human counterparts. And no, we don't mean the birth pangs (this book will spare you such details), but the tendency of those surrounding the couple to take an inordinate interest in the affairs of the child, at times even rivalling the parents' enthusiasm.

Everybody wants a say: the child's name, hairstyle, school, and, among more conservative cultures, the choice of friends, spouse and eventual profession. Here we recall an interesting case study by Johnson & Johnson, titled "Hello My Name Means". They overturned a name's cultural associations with real-world data on its contemporary associations. They drew and presented this data contextually for each name, using Twitter for which subjects most interested those of a certain name, Last.fm for their choice in music, LinkedIn for the most common profession, and so on, giving every name a unique board that was updated in real time. One can already see the applications for such a solution for midwives in the Marteching™ profession.

Like we said, no sooner is the baby out, than everyone's remarking at a feature or a trait, going "Did you see his reflexes? He'll be a squash player." Likewise, it's the same in Martech. Everyone has an opinion on what it's going to grow up to be. You'll know this from every conference or roundtable you've ever attended, seeing the same clichés circulating for well over a decade now: convergence, innovation, customisation, personalisation, hyper-personalisation. You know the drill.

But ask a Martecher? Boy, things look different from the inside.

The goal is in sight, the ball is at your feet, and you know it kills you to shrink the gap. But that's why you're in these shoes. Somebody somewhere believes that you can deliver, even if that somebody is only you.

Like the C-word that defined the CMO as minister, there is another C-word defining the CMO as midwife, and that is–wait for it–CORD.

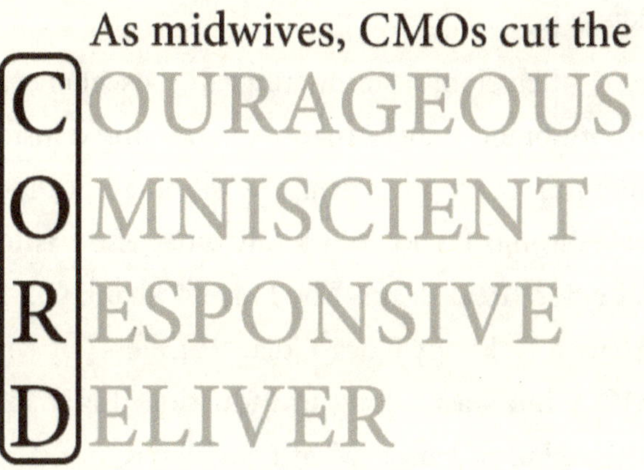

The CMO is selected from among the most courageous, omniscient, responsive ones who can deliver. In short, cut the CORD. Allow us to present 4 from among the very top-notch marketing midwives.

Courage

Marc Pritchard, Procter & Gamble's Chief Brand Officer, can teach us a thing or two about courage. In 2018, on the back of serious ad fraud concerns expressed by himself and a few other courageous CMOs, he announced a $200 million budget cut–you read that right, a cut–in digital ad spends. An advocate for the use of marketing tech in driving growth and innovation, he literally put his money where his mouth was. The result? The bet paid off. Wastage and fraud went down, trust and transparency went up, and sales went up, up, up. Now who wouldn't want a Marc Pritchard on his team?

Omniscience

Diversity, inclusion, multicultural excellence, social responsibility, brand transformation, marketing transformation, not to mention iconic advertising. What do all of these have in common? Antonio Lucio. You know what else has to do with Antonio Lucio? "Real Beauty" by Dove, "Thank you Mom" by P&G, "Share a Coke" by Coca-Cola, "Priceless" by Mastercard. The CMO Club wasn't long in inducting this man of many hats in their Hall of Fame. What next? We're not sure, but it's definitely under his sleeve.

Responsive

Everybody wants to pivot, but not everyone can pull it off. Here's one man who's done it, and how: Jerry Stritzke, the CEO of REI, a leading outdoor retail brand in America. Rather than pander to the Black Friday craze, Jerry incentivised his employees to take the day off, and spend it outdoors instead. So, they shut their stores every Black Friday, beginning 2015. Two things happened. First, sales went UP. Second, the move kicked off a movement, with 170 national, state, and local organisations, and more than 2.7 million people joining in. REI keeps up their tradition to this day, even extending it beyond Black Friday. When they zig you zag, as the saying goes.

Deliver

There are CMOs and there are CMOs. Sometimes, what separates the men from the boys is the women. Women like Alicia Tillman, current CMO at Capitolis Inc. Before that, she led brand transformation at SAP, digital transformation at American Express, pioneered Ariba's first-ever customer loyalty program, Sun Microsystems' first-ever customer advisory board and globally scaled up the i2 Technologies brand preceding its acquisition. But delivering stellar brand performance isn't all she does. As a board member for the nonprofit "Girls Who Code", she's worked on delivering technology from the gender gap. How does she do it? Beats us. No wonder Forbes named her one of the "World's Most Influential CMOs" in 2021.

Are we overselling it? Being marketers ourselves, are we attributing a bit too much of an organisation's success to the department we work in? Perhaps. But if we're guilty, let us be guilty of celebrating Marketing, and not the Marketer.

Think for a moment of the companies on today's Fortune 500 list which weren't even public a decade ago: Uber, Alibaba, Meta. Could they have gotten there without offering great products or services, powerfully sold? It's what marketers do.

And, think of the companies on today's Fortune 50 list that WERE here a decade ago: Walmart, Apple, AT&T. What did they get right? You'd be remiss not to mention Marketing.

You see, cutting that CORD isn't an easy day's work. It takes finding the right people, putting them in the right place, equipping them to do the right thing, and then watching it happen. That's Management 101. But more on that in the next chapter.

~ ~ ~ ~

Chapter 8

Marteching™ Departments as Manager

More than a dozen years and as many CMOs ago, before there was such a thing as Google Maps on your mobile phone, Dominos' US agency Crispin Porter + Bogusky created the Knock Box. What was the Knock Box? From the outside, a plain old Dominos pizza box, but made from industrial elements, instead of cardboard. The inside was a whole other story. A simple knock-knock would dial the nearest Dominos outlet via an embedded sim, and take your order via speakerphone. Within 30 minutes you'd be tucking into a hot pizza whether you were in a parked car, on a park bench or at a nice, quiet hideaway.

How did that happen? Process. Innovative process, to be precise. You see, the + sign in the agency's name meant the addition of Bogusky, an industrial designer, who introduced this harebrained idea: "We ought to brief the industrial design team at the same time as the creative team." So, while the creatives zipped off to crack a communication strategy, his designers worked on a product strategy.

Until Alex Bogusky introduced that process, the total number of agencies practising it were precisely zero. Remember **People**, **Process** and **Practice** from a few chapters ago? Notice now, how important "People" is, and why it must come first?

That '+' sign between Crispin Porter and Bogusky reminded us of another innovative '+': the "Copy + Art" duo. Who came up with that process? They don't teach this in advertising courses, or bring it up on the shop floor, but the genius behind that idea is someone all of Adland is familiar with for several other reasons: William Bernbach. Until he introduced the simple yet unheard of process, that copywriter and art director ought to work as a 2-member team, it just wasn't done. Most agencies, the copywriter cracked the idea with the "suits"–slang for the account manager, who ran the account (aka client)–and then handed it over to the art department, to make something of it.

But we're putting the cart before the horse; discussing Advertising in a Marketing chapter. So let's back it up a bit. What was this chapter called? Right: "*Marteching™ Departments as Manager*". And seeing as we're going with an unconventional spelling of "marketing", perhaps the time is now ripe to tell you why that is.

You see, we believe Marketing has transformed forever. Yes, we hear that said about 20 times before lunch, and we may even roll our eyes at it. But hear us out. Who creates technology? Is it us marketers? Of course not. Is it the customer? Hardly. Who, then? The engineer. It is the engineer's job to assemble–at times create–the nuts and bolts that comprise the technology we marvel at today. But there's a catch. As brilliant as these minds may be, they are in most cases not native to the domain in which their product or service will be used and experienced.

There is no greater example of this than the marketing dashboards of half a decade ago: remember what they were like? Clunky, distracted, pinball-esque monstrosities that we all secretly wished would go away. And (for the most part) they have. Why didn't they work? We wonder. But why wonder? Think: as a marketer, don't you instinctively know what you'd rather have the dashboard feature? Yes you would, and you'd have the particulars ready in an instant. And why is that? Because this is your domain. So, if the engineer were to put on the Marketer's hat, would he not make more intuitive dashboards? Logically, yes.

But that is more easily said than done. And this is why, for all that talk of Marketing Transformation, we know that nothing will truly transform if the little details aren't right. Finally, over the latter part of the last decade, those little details have started to get right. Maybe engineers have begun taking stretch assignments. Maybe the smartest marketers have switched over to the tech side. We don't know what it is. But we can tell that marketing technology has now come into its own, allowing us to safely place "marketing" as an artefact of the past, to be replaced with Marteching™ (since marketing can no longer exist without its better half, technology). So, it is useless to speak of Marketing and Martech, as if they were somehow mutually exclusive things. The twain have matched, they have met, and now they are married. (And if you're curious as to why we placed "match" before "met", meet the Tinder generation.)

Let's get back to **People**, **Process** and **Practice**. Thumb back to chapter 3, where we laid it all out. Recall that we'd said "none of this (i.e., cutting edge Marteching™ practice) takes place by chance, but by design"?

This chapter will lay out the design.

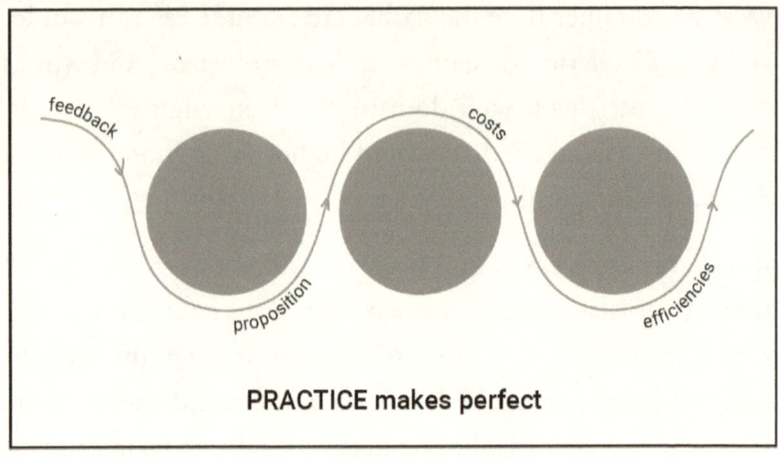

PRACTICE makes perfect

We will do so by revisiting the entry and exit points in the "Practice makes Perfect" diagram. The incoming elements could be feedback from an ongoing campaign, competitor information, a government policy update, a budgetary constraint, and so on. What happens next is Marteching™ gets its hands on it, and turns it to its advantage, before sending it out again. And what's being sent out? Improvements: a more intuitive, competitive, up-to-date and lean campaign, for one. Now if this sounds like all in a day's work, you should know it isn't. So what does it take? Well, you've heard it before: **People**, **Process** and **Practice**. In THAT order.

Let's break it down here.

Let's take the scenario of a campaign. And let's say we're dealing with a service this time. What say we take something in fintech? Let's say the brand is an established player in financial services, who've usually kept their end up against entrenched players, but have begun ceding ground to fintech upstarts.

The purpose of this campaign, as any, is to grow their customer base. However, the mushrooming of upstarts in the fintech space has been cause for much consternation, with some entrenched players engaging in knee-jerk tactics, sending confusing signals to their counterparts. And so, in the case we will examine, your brand's arch rival has roped in a celebrity, whose relevance and vivacity could grow their audience and market share by several basis points. What do you do? "Wait-and-watch" is not on the cards. As the head of Marketing, you HAVE to go live with your campaign, or else.

Ready? Let's begin. We start on a Monday morning. It's about 8AM, and you receive the <ding> of a notification. You see the tiny logo of your organisation's collaborative software–let's call it Slick. You're about to dismiss it, mistaking it for another recurring weekly reminder for some team meet or other. But it isn't. It's an email. Subject line: "Did you see this???" You groan inwardly. Not at the 3 question marks, but that it's from your equal number in Sales, who you recall (as you groan again) knows his stuff. The in-app video plays seamlessly, and you wonder why the internet is only sketchy when you're watching something interesting.

But then you lean forward. The video is an ad for a competitor, let's call them Brand Y. You've never seen this ad before, and you wonder why: your automated competitive intelligence tool has always kept you well informed ahead of most. Why the lag now? You return to the email, and notice he left a link: a landing page for Brand Y's website. How thoughtful. You click, and notice the campaign literally just went live less than an hour ago.

Their hashtag rings a bell. You thumb over to an unread email titled: "Brand Y Signs Up Celebrity A", which you'd left unopened thinking, "Let them waste their money… celebs won't bring the authenticity this category needs." Or so you'd thought. And now, you have second thoughts.

In between the cereal and the elevator, you send 1 channel message and 3 direct messages, and wait for the reactions. Why won't this app permit read receipts, you ask frustratingly, as you get into the car. You hear a ding. Was that a notification? No, just the seat belt alarm. You strap yourself in. Take a deep breath. It's going to be one long day.

You adjust your mirror: "What were they thinking, signing Celeb X on. Wouldn't his daughter have made a better choice? She is, after all, a young entrepreneur and fintech influencer on Instagram. What'd she have–a million followers? Or was that views?" You rouse your sleepy car voice assistant: "Tell me…" it bleeps to attention. "…does Influencer X have a million followers on her Instagram? Or was that YouTube views…" The answer doesn't surprise you. She's big on Instagram. Perfect for your brand, isn't it? You're all about snackable content. You collaborate with her over the big piece, and then let the micro- and nano-influencers break it down from there across channels.

You start the car, and as it idles, you receive a notification: a channel message, from hands down the smartest member of your team. "What does Celeb X get about this category? Isn't his daughter the one with that snazzy new fintech prototype we've been eying?" This girl is due a promotion. Make that a double. Of COURSE it's a perfect fit. Not just the father-daughter angle, not even the generational angle. She's actually floated a fintech prototype our product guys have been eying.

Could a collaboration be far off? We've got to get our foot in the door. "Now", you say aloud, as you take your foot off the pedal, unstrap yourself, and heave your way out. What was the name of her chatbot? Ah, it'll come to me.

Your excitement cannot contain itself. It's a work from home day, you think, jubilantly, as you bound up the 3 flights home. You open up your workstation. No new notifications. No problem. You schedule a huddle in 15 minutes. They feel like 45. At last, the team's in, the ones who count, anyway, and you begin. It's an audio-only call, but the reactions indicate the enthusiasm has now escalated to level: Video. You switch to see their beaming faces, they can see yours, and almost read your mind. "So what you're saying is…" goes Shweta of the Double Promo, "We sign her up. THIS week. And go live next Monday?" You can hear a pin drop. The energy is palpable. They know the answer is "yes", but they want to hear you say it. Complications abound. Your campaign is days away from go-live. The agency will throw a fit–who wouldn't?–but you won't throw in the towel. You have your strategy ready. When they say "We can't change the campaign at the last minute," you respond with: "They will shelve their campaign within a week, wasting all that media spend–they even have a roadblock planned." And now, you give them the bait: "Think of the haul at the award shows: media, creative, effectiveness. I'll sponsor half the team tickets." There's a pause at the other end, and you know they know they're beat. The Creative Director caves. In comes a "mindblown" sticker reaction from the junior copywriter. They exchange glances, and tell you they'll come back to you by EoD with something solid. You say you knew they would.

You check the clock. It's not yet 11AM. Ample time for the talent agency to be up and about. You make the phone call. Cut to a whole day and many push notifications, voice calls, private chats and emojis later, you have what you need: a signed contract between brand and celebrity. She sounded even more excited about the idea than you did, and for some reason, believed her dad would be, too. He was paid, he delivered. So what if a rival brand used their street smarts to outsmart his endorsement? He'd just as soon endorse a rival once his contract expired–no loyalty there. And the way they saw it, the Dad vs Daughter standoff could lead to great buzz for them both, and who wouldn't want that.

So that was that.

What you just saw was a flawless performance involving People, Process and Practice, and at no point was marketing technology absent from the interface between people, between processes, and between people and process. As we will see in the next chapter, technology can be the glue that holds silos together.

~ ~ ~ ~

Chapter 9

Working around Silos

Where did silos get all the negative press? Aren't silos necessary for a culture? When we look at the etymology of the word itself, we see that it connotes a dugout: a cave or shelter for the storage of crops or grain. Now why should we be breaking those down?

Perhaps "breaking down silos" worked for the open-plan brigade, who saw demonising private work spaces as an opportunity to introduce their flat architectural solution? Perhaps.

And this is where our central theme of the "marriage" of Marketing and Tech comes to our aid, because just as space is key to the wellbeing of equals living as one, so it is with working relationships. Too little space, and the relationship wears. Too much and it withers.

Johan Cruyff, the proponent of the winning phenomenon "Total Football" that saw Dutch domination of the sport in the 1970s explained it this way: it was the perfect combination of player movement, coordination, and spacing. There's that word again. Why is spacing so important? We will come back to Johan Cruyff and Total Football in a few chapters, but first, let us dedicate some "space" to the pressing silo question.

Strategically speaking, there are 3 functional divisions in Marteching™: Technology, Data and Content, bound together by the Management layer. Technology is the infrastructure, Data the lifeblood and Content the heart producing the bits and bytes that attract and grow the business. These demarcations create silos at the primary level: the strategic.

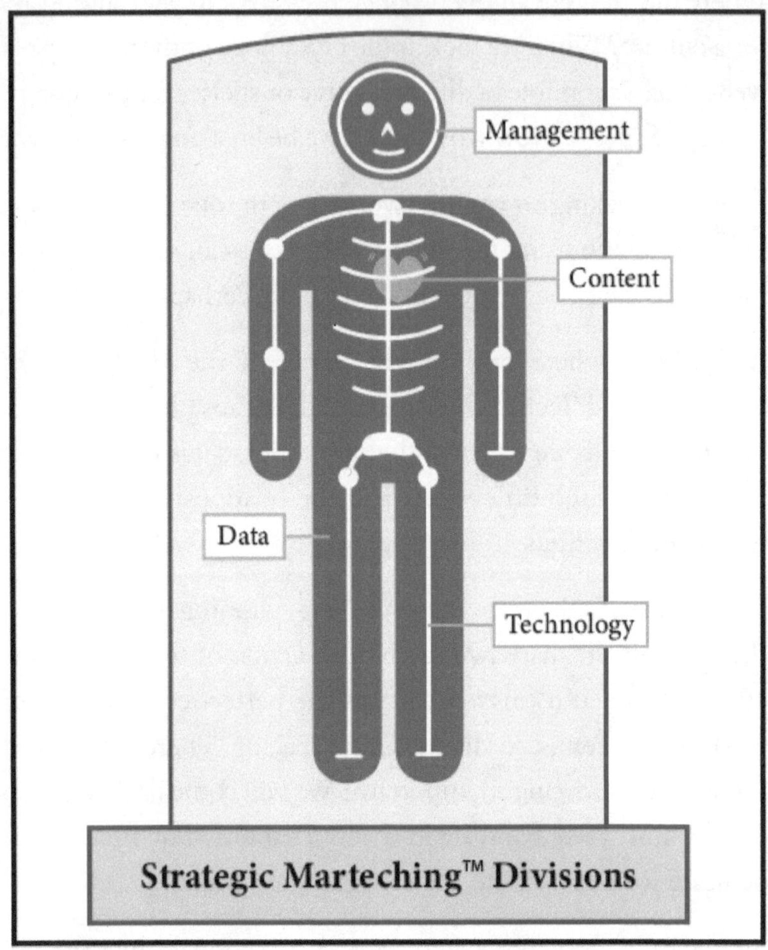

Operationally speaking, there are 5: Strategy, Content Creation, Media Distribution, Customer Experience and Data & Analytics. They work a lot like Michael Porter's classic value chain, with 2 key differences: (1) the model is cyclic, not linear; and (2) silo 5 feeds back into silo 1. These demarcations create silos at the secondary level: the operational.

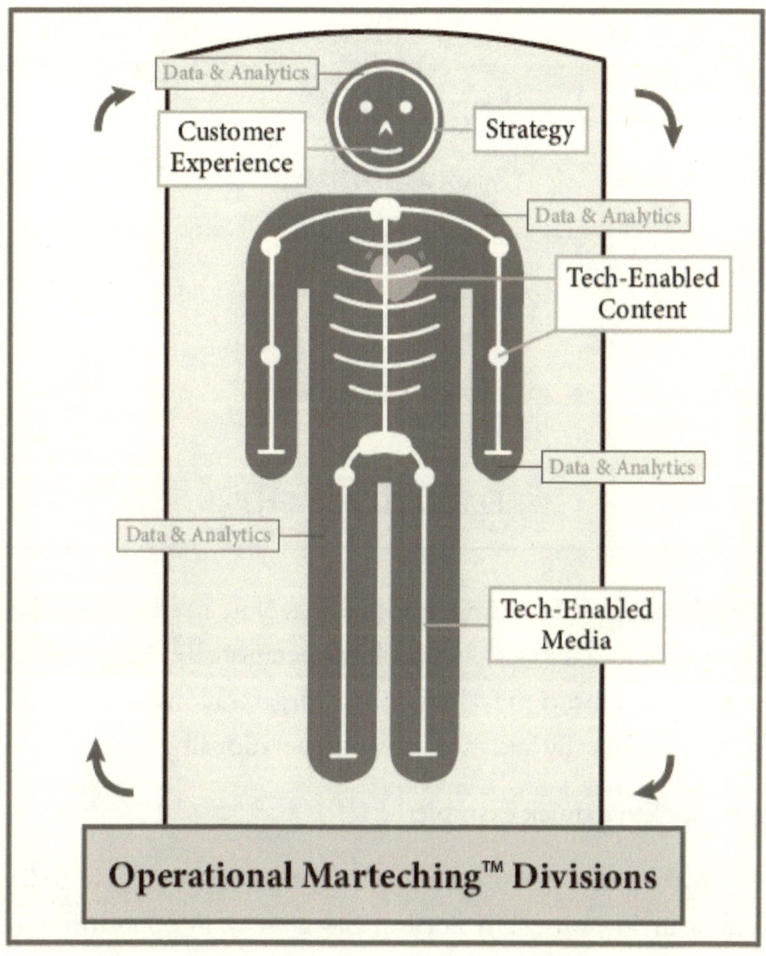

Here's what that flow looks like when you add each department's role.

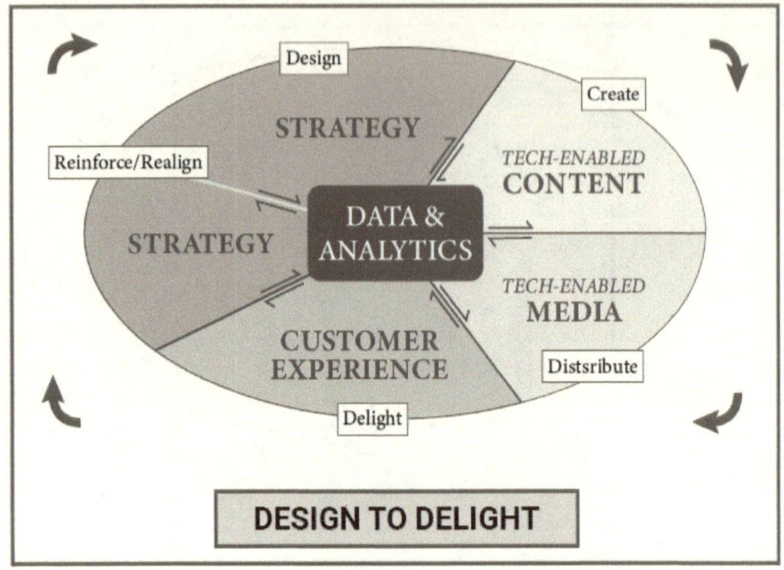

The key–and this is important–is that you need more space between silos strategically, and less operationally. The tragedy–and this is all too prevalent–is that organisations are way too siloed strategically and even *more* so operationally.

Let's look at a quick example:

Say you have a sales promotion campaign that went live today, and your in-house UX Analyst Simar sees an opportunity to increase conversions. He needs to tell the signal from the noise, and so, decides to test between 2 user experiences: which one would lead to more conversions? However, the campaign's short time span means he can't wait around for the test to return something of statistical significance (which typically happens with A/B testing.) And so, in the interest of time and conversions, he decides to deploy an algorithm designed to gauge the better performing content asset and serve more of it, without having to check with home base. And there is the catch. Home Base is run by Data Ops, with their own protocols. To them, a few customers lost during testing is not too high a cost to pay to arrive at a sane, testable and implementable result. Cost of doing business, they'd shrug. But, the clock is running out for Simar.

See the problem? Strategically speaking, great to have that padding between silos. After all, with just the right space, it CAN produce sane, testable and implementable results, leading to a competitive advantage. But operationally speaking, it could be a nightmare.

And here we would like to introduce this graph posited by Rob Goffee and Gareth Jones in 1996.

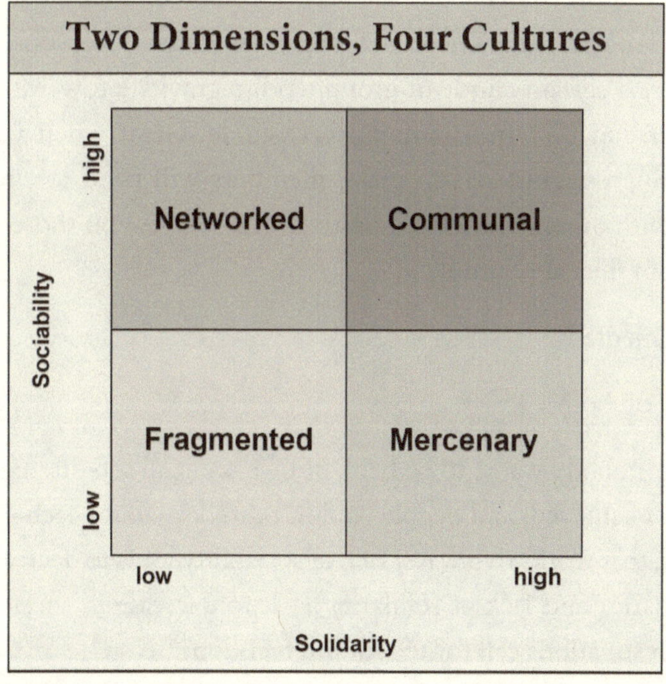

They plotted the cultural coordinates of an organisation, function or team against two attributes: sociability and solidarity.

They defined sociability as the degree of genuine friendship among members of a group, and solidarity as the degree to which a group's members come together to achieve common goals irrespective of that friendship.

To help you decode this further, here are a few examples for each quadrant. And remember, this graph needn't only indicate *within* team culture, but even *between* team culture, which is more the point of this chapter.

Networked:

High on Sociability, Low on Solidarity

A young startup where not everyone knows everyone, but where a certain clique or group tend to gravitate towards each other and hire from among their circle. Great when you're starting out, but as you grow, members will need to cut the ice with others in the organisation, and rely less on those with whom they are familiar.

Fragmented:

Low on both

Well, nobody wants to be here, but we see it all too often: goals aren't achieved, and people couldn't care less about each other. And, that works two ways: lack of sociability leads to decrease in solidarity, and lack of solidarity leads to decrease in sociability. Such situations call for urgent intervention.

Mercenary:

Low on Sociability, High on Solidarity

How, you may wonder, might Mercenary groups excel in achieving their common goals in the absence of genuine friendship among each other? Think about doctors or nurses. Need they know each other in order to save a life on the operating table? Definitely not. It may help, but it is not necessary. Here's a sign of mercenary culture: when a member introduces themselves socially with "I'm a Data Analyst", omitting to mention the organisation or function (Marketing).

Communal:

High on both

Now who wouldn't aspire to be here? Imagine being a team, function or an organisation in need of communal culture, and actually getting there, and staying there. In their heyday, you would plot organisations like Zappos or w00t smack dab centre here. Of course, "Communal" isn't for everyone, and even those benefiting from it find sustenance untenable, often for good reason. (You do after all want to achieve your common goals even in the absence of genuine friendship between members.) Here's a sign of Communal culture: when a member introduces themselves socially with "I work at Apple", followed by "I'm a Build Engineer."

Think of every organisation, function or team you've ever worked in. Try and plot them on this graph. You may discover that you're plotting your team in one quadrant, and your organisation in another. Or, your local function in one, and the international function in another. Or, more central to our discussion in this chapter, the Marketing department in one, and Technology in another. What a tragedy this can be.

But there is hope. Return to that graph, and recall where you'd placed your team, function or organisation. Let's do this exercise with just one. Say it's a Marketing team. Here's what you've got to remember. The position you allotted them on the graph is static. It's a cross-sectional view on where things stand today. But where do you want to direct them? Isn't that part of your KRA? Alright, so plot that point out. Give it a horizon of 2 years. So if the first one is titled Sep 2023, title the next one Sep 2025.

See what you did there? You drew a vector. A direction. That's the essence of strategy. You have a starting point, and an endpoint. Now, look at that vector: doesn't it forecast better things? Along this vector you will plot all the actions that you plan on introducing, in order to take your team from here to there: hiring, training, SCRUM-ing, team building, recreation. That's your department. And, you will use this very vector to plan and upsell your budget. How about that? One little vector, so many positive outcomes.

Now of course, you cannot change culture without changing structure. So, if you wish to shift your culture towards one of collaboration, you're going to need a more collaborative structure. When you glance at how organisations are structured in Michael Porter's value chain model, you will immediately notice one change you will wish to make: move Tech out of support and into core: more specifically, into Operations. And it's not just you. Today, every organisation must examine itself: "Do we view Technology as core to our business? Or is it a support function?"

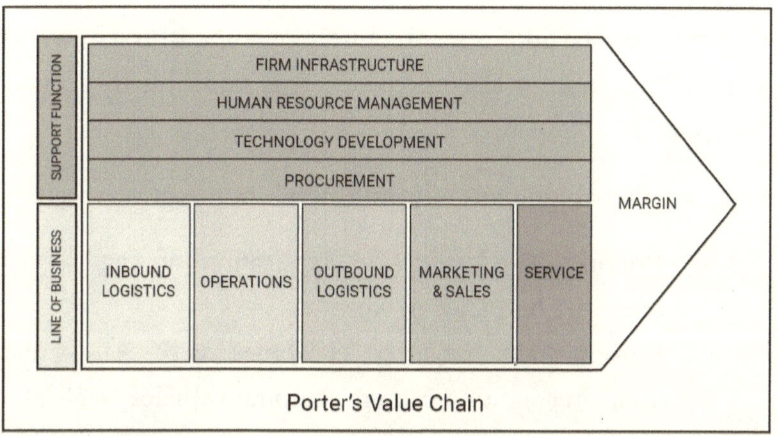

Porter's Value Chain

If there's anything we've learned over the past decade or two of Martech's ascent, it is this: no matter which sector we work in, we ALL work in Technology. Think of a brand like Netflix. Sure, it's in the Media & Entertainment sector, but one whiff of that black-box recommendation algorithm, and you're not so certain: is it a tech brand? Entertainment brand? Ditto for Spotify. Think of Uber, Ikea, or Amazon. Or, of late, Walmart. Which sector (or sectors) do they operate in? No matter which, you will notice Technology is as core to their business as their core value proposition.

And here, we drop a name you wouldn't expect to hear in this context: John Deere. The tractor brand? Yes, the tractor brand. Surely we didn't mean Tesla? No, John Deere, the American agricultural auto major, ranking among the Global Fortune 100s.

Thinking of John Deere and technology may make you go "Ah, this must have to do with their engineering department–they're tech savvy," or maybe you're wondering "Could they have bought an expensive piece of software?" And this is where we're starting to see Technology come into its own as a "core" function in a sector where it is traditionally seen as "support".

Here are a few highlights of John Deere's home-grown tech:

- Robotics-based precision application of fertiliser to seed, and herbicide to weed
- Autonomous harvester combines with AI-assisted image recognition cameras helping vehicles "see", and farm managers interpret data
- IoT & cloud-enabled tractors relaying 2,000 sensor measurements/second PER machine

To put that last point into context: Twitter processes an average of 6,000 tweets a second. John Deere–the tractor company–is processing a third of that every second PER machine. Multiply that by the number of operable machines, and you're talking 10-15 million measurements a second.

Just a decade ago they were installing telematics gateways in every piece of large equipment; today they're attracting top Silicon Valley talent. Quite the harvest. What we have here is more than just smart farming, or agtech. We're looking at the pioneering of Agriculture 4.0.

Now, do you still see John Deere as a tractor company?

So, to return to the point we were making, before we understand silos, we need to understand the role of Tech in today's companies and the value it brings.

As we said, there are two ways Tech influences organisations: as a support function and as core.

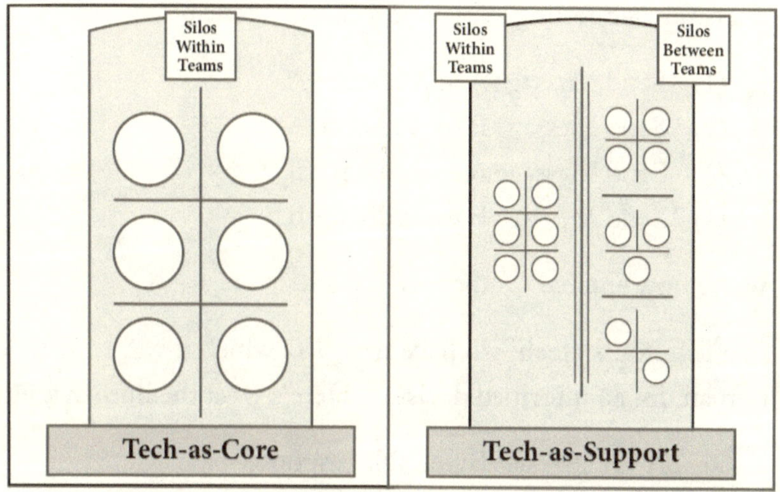

Technology as a Core Function

At first glance, in organisations where Technology is a core function, it would occupy a position in Operations. But that isn't the case. Remember when we pointed out non-tech companies held together by the glue that is Technology?

You will see that at work when Tech is a core function. But here, we must introduce the second silo: Data. In it bounds, into the inbound logistics box, where it is first processed by a Martech solution. We open the package. What does it contain? A user-insight with an audience cohort of 3,200, give or take. If we respond within 'x' time, we will reap 'y' reward. The decision takes microseconds, because we're dealing with an automated solution built by intelligent humans for speed and scale. The decision is made, and we move over to the Operations box. What do we find? Tech at work, once again. This time, before we've blinked, it's breezed through the list of related digital assets, shortlisted 2, extracted and bifurcated the audience into 2 sets for A-B testing, and done 4 things at once.

(1) Send Message A to Audience A
(2) Send Message B to Audience A
(3) Send Message A to Audience B
(4) Send Message B to Audience B

We've now entered Outbound Logistics.

In a few hours, Tech will have user data which it will relay to a human, for an informed decision. Here's what the human sees:

1. A→A 48% net favourable response
2. B→A 63% net favourable response
3. A→B 30% net favourable response
4. B→B 85% net favourable response

Clearly, Message B is better favoured by both audiences, and Audience B is the low hanging fruit. What's the call? Option 2? Option 4? Both? Tech awaits, patiently. The human decides: "Go with option 4", and sets an automated instruction for "Permit option 2 with threshold 75%".

Tech does the rest. It's created lookalikes from the initial sample of 3,200, bifurcated the larger set once again into Audience B and A, and initiated the sequence of communication. Now how hard was that? Actually, very. And could any of this have taken place with there being lack of communication between silos? Quite impossible.

And this is one of the reasons why the above case today is very infrequently to be found in the hallways of Martech even among the best of adtech solutions. Why is that? For one, the lack of cross-domain knowledge among engineers creating Martech solutions, something we lamented in the previous chapter.

But all of that is changing. Just as John Deere is hiring top Silicon Valley talent, Martech too is seeing an inflow of media professionals co-creating adtech solutions. Who ought to "wear the pants"? Well, we gave away that answer in the very first chapter, itself: Marketing. This is Marketing Ops, after all.

Let us now look at organisations where Technology is a support function.

Technology as a Support Function

This is where silos can truly hinder various departments in an organisation from achieving a common goal. As corporate woes go, they don't get bigger than this. The reason is simple: Marketing is the growth department. You grow or you die. When an organisation's structure places Tech at the periphery of all the action, that stymies growth. Put Tech in the thick of the action, and you stimulate growth. But the ground is shifting as value shifts from the legacy "tech as support" model to "tech as core" model of an organisation's dynamics. It's pivot or perish.

As we've seen, "Tech as core" comes with its share of challenges, with silos within teams. But "tech as support" exacerbates them.

What's the workaround?

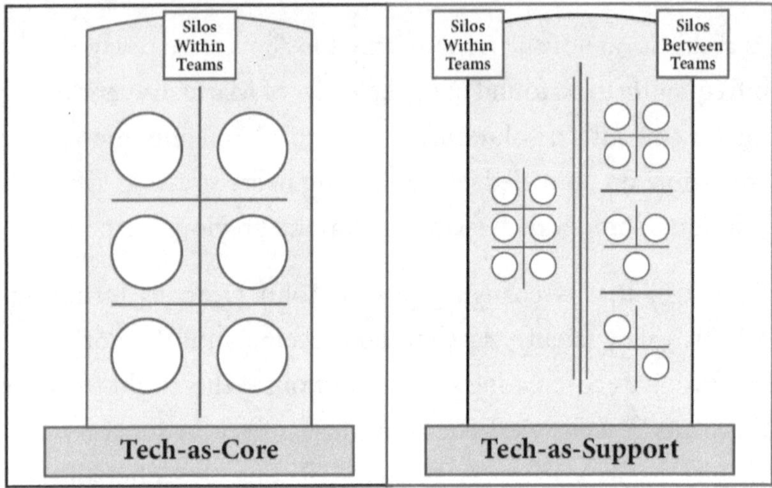

Let's revisit our silo graph as we unpack the answer.

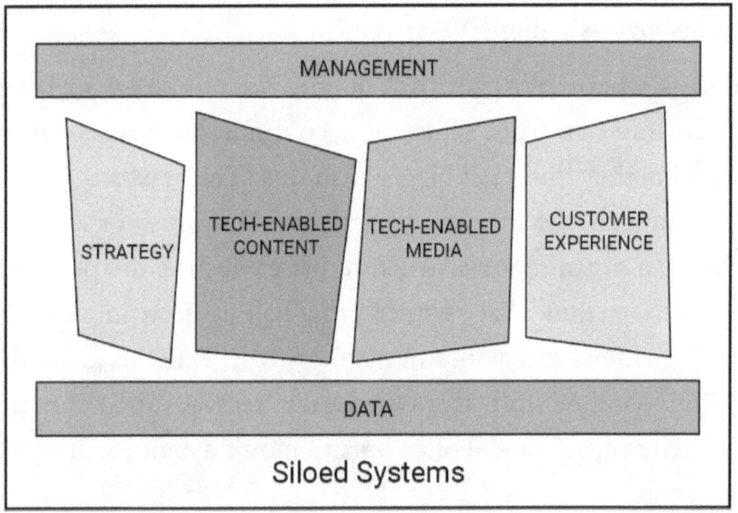

The key here is proximity. The divisions you see here are placed in this proximity to each other, in the organisation. Do you see a problem? It has "silo" baked into the very structure itself. The answer? Marteching™: a Marketing-owned function combining strategy and operations, drawing from the various disciplines at its disposal: analytics, automation, aggregation, the list is thick as a marketing stack.

Visualise folds. They are a great way to organise while retaining the unity of the entity. When stored away (think strategy), your siloes are compartmentalised. But when in utilisation (think operations), they are a single piece of fabric, again.

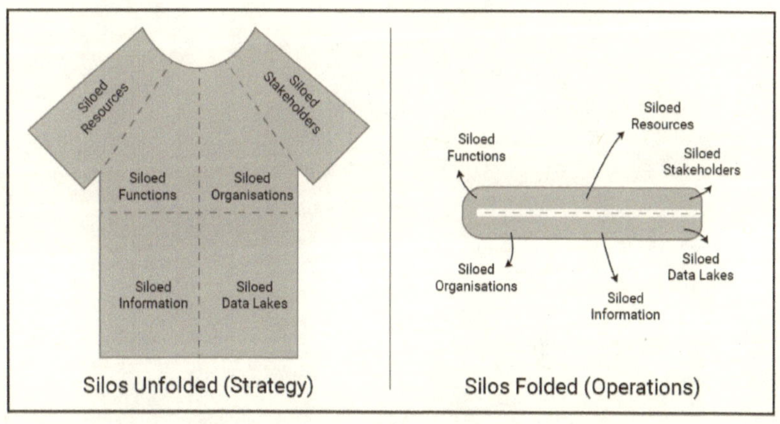

~ ~ ~ ~

Chapter 10

Healthy Relationships Yield Value

We've now reached the book's halfway point. And, that's the perfect point to take a quick pit stop, and rest our faculties for a while. While you stretch out your legs and order a refreshing drink, we'll do a quick recap.

If you flip the book over, you will see an image of an airborne car flying newlyweds off to their honeymoon. Of course, we know that life isn't a honeymoon, which is why we wrote an entire book beneath that cover. The first few chapters established and then expanded on the idea of Marketing and Technology being two parties in a binding relationship. Marketing is the discipline; Tech the enabler. We saw the two introduce themselves, tell their history, gravitate towards the compatible qualities in the other, and now, we've begun to watch them navigate the nitty gritties of everyday married life.

This chapter deals with how this couple—by which we mean Martech—can eke the most of their relationship, and how only long-term healthy relationships can return this value.

Let's look at the various aspects of running a home, and we'll find all the fodder we need to keep our Martech relationships on a steady footing. We will get granular in upcoming chapters, but for now, will keep things more or less general.

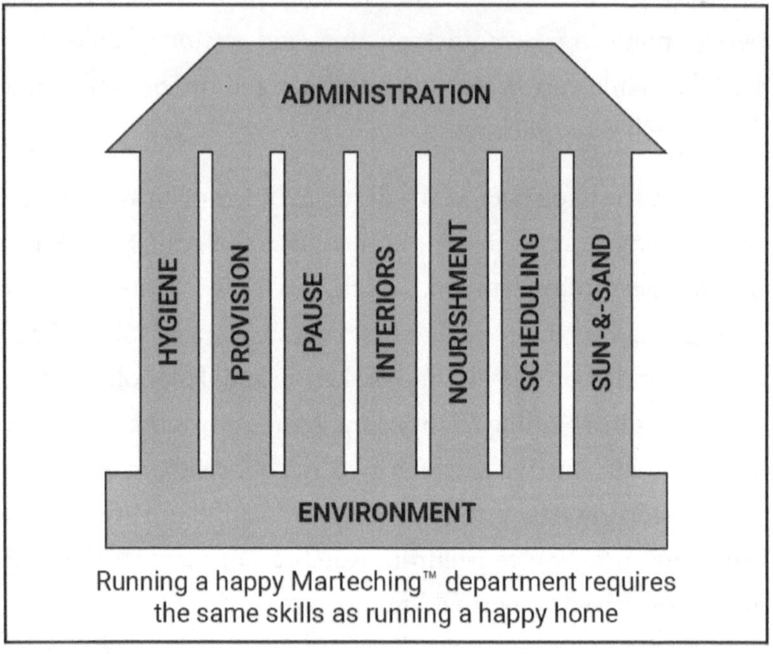

Running a happy Marteching™ department requires the same skills as running a happy home

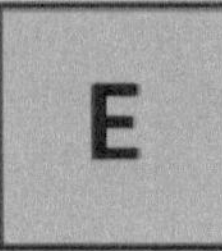

Environment

The environment of a home is two-fold: within as well as beyond its walls. To begin with, a homemaker plans where they will build that home not from internals, but externals: what environment will best suit the family? What location is placed most conveniently near the best schools, hospitals, markets and in some cases, loved ones?

Planning a Marteching™ department is no different. The chief Martecher must plan their own department beginning not with internals, but externals. They must first give consideration to where their industry, sector, market and consumer is poised and headed, and not to their own team/function/organisation's culture. Culture, after all, is a response, not a cause.

Here, a Martecher will tailor their choices according to the environment they're in. A B2B company will operate in a different environment from B2C, for example. A startup will operate in a different ecosystem from an MNC. Where a homemaker may've weighed location, a Martecher weighs proximities: should my Data Ops team sit adjacent to Tech Ops? Or Marketing Ops? Should I build an independent Martech stack? Or should we pick and choose from among the enterprise stack, and fill in the gaps?

Hidden within these assumptions and answers is value, waiting to be unlocked. Which makes choosing the right environment a most worthy endeavour. And a risky one, too, prompting the cautious Martecher to rent in the area before choosing to buy a home there.

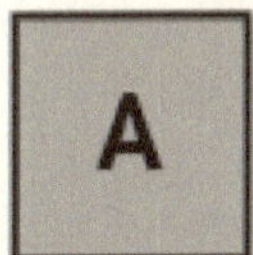

Administration

Once you've moved in, you've got to run the place. And, as homemakers quickly find out, it takes more than 2 to run a home these days. Depending on where they live, modern families call on the assistance of a cook, maidservant, babysitter, gardener, gatekeeper, and so on. First, you have to find the right talent, and often train them for the job they've been hired to do.

The latter point is a crucial one for today's Martecher, since there is virtually nobody with Marteching™ experience to be found. Where would you find a Martecher with 20 years experience in a field that isn't that old? You have to improvise. As with recruiting for the home, the astute Martecher seeks will over skill. You can always train someone's skill; but you can never train their will. They either *will* or they won't.

Before we move on to the next area, think for a moment about the various aspects of running a home. Ought a homemaker need to know how to cook, when recruiting a cook? It helps, doesn't it? A polite cook could turn pesky, upon discovering a lack of domain experience in the one hiring them. And so it is in Marteching™, too. No, you needn't be an expert in home gardening, but cross-domain knowledge can go a long way in keeping you in the driving seat of the affairs that drive your home—or in the Martecher's case, your department.

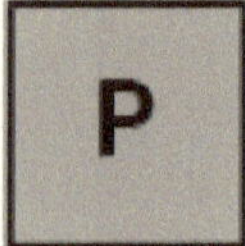

Provision

Next up, providing for the home. Right from day 1 you're going to need food, groceries, utilities and other peripherals required to run a home. This is where couples often complement each other, one being great with the budget, the other with the bargain. You ideally want both. In the Marteching™ sense, you want your budget and your buys to balance each other. Too far within and you'll be undernourished, too much beyond and you'll be overspending.

What will you be spending on? Often, just as with a home, things that are the cost of running a home: the cost of doing business. Here is where we must stress an important point. Somewhere during the last century, well after today's large, global organisations began to be entrenched, they began to see Marketing as a cost. We've already noted in Michael Porter's value chain, that Technology has traditionally been seen as a cost, being a support function. But can we say that anymore for Technology? And could we *ever* have said that for Marketing? Never forget that Marketing—and now Marteching™ is the "Growth" department of every organisation.

So no, growth isn't a cost of doing business any more than providing for your family is; it is its very purpose. And therefore, the Martecher's job is to ensure that their Marteching™ investments will induce growth, and not groans, in their organisation.

Nourishment

Who prepares the nourishment at your home? A spouse? A parent? You may have both in your home, and yet, they may not always choose to work the pots and pans. Often times you may order in. Or, choose to go out. Or perhaps you're among the homes that have recruited a cook whose talent outshines that of the homeowners.

Take this analogy without missing a beat, to Marteching™. Ought you to be a master of all? Surely, not. Who can? Yes, a modicum of awareness on how a tool works, or what a solution does, is necessary for any Martecher. But oftentimes, you're best left dealing with an expert beyond your confines, who will bring the value you can't, for a fair price.

Think of all the avenues for nourishment in your department. A data enrichment layer on your website could greatly elevate your CRM performance. A sprinkle of AI in your media planning would add a dash of flavour to your content marketing. You *know* this. But how do you get it done? You bring in the experts, and let them show you how it's done. This is your show, but that is their domain.

And this is a notable point to make, since these days, much of the "pizzazz" in Marteching™ is brought by tools built for a specific purpose by domain experts who know exactly how to wield them. There's no point you being the ringmaster *and* wanting to work the trapeze. Set your limits, work with the best, and you'll see wonders take place.

Interior Design

Now, think of your home's interiors: rooms, furniture, storage, aesthetics. Are there lessons here for Marteching™? You bet there are. Let's begin with rooms. What happens there? Well, to each room its own activity. You don't do bathroom stuff in the kitchen, or bedroom stuff out on the balcony. Likewise, in the Marteching™ department, you carve out "rooms". These are the silos we mentioned in the previous chapter. Each room also represents a mindset, wherein to conduct the activity appropriate to it.

Next, furniture. Stuff to sit on, stand around and store things in. It's about aesthetics and application. Form and function. So what does *your* Marteching™ layout look like? What arrangement could you make, that would facilitate the smoothest navigation within and between rooms? Do your storage items—think Data—remain stowed away in storage? If you were to look for something, would you be able to find it? These are questions you must address immediately, since the answers are quick and easy, permitting a recalibration of a process or retrieval of data on the go.

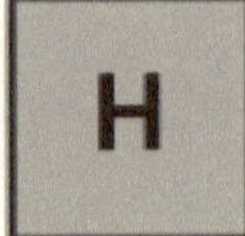

Hygiene

Could you run your home long without subjecting it to a thorough cleaning? Surely, not. The best way to do it of course, is to *keep* it clean. How do you do that? Great question. First step: with clean practices—don't litter. Think about the many times you may leave your dirty socks around, or throw the trash in the wrong can. It happens. Happens to the best of us. But that is why hygiene is a never-ending job. There is no finite beginning and end to it.

It's the same way with Marteching™. You *want* clean processes; you *want* cleaner data. The best way to go about it is to start clean, and avoid messing things up. And then, you're going to need regular sprucing up sessions, and the annual spring clean.

One of the good things about deep cleaning is you often discover long-lost treasure behind the sofa or under the bed. It's the same with Marteching™. Maybe your spring clean involved a team outbound, where you discovered an insight that led to unearthing a rich data asset that was just sitting there unused. It's amazing what you can achieve when you just pick up a broom to clear up the cobwebs.

So, keep things neat and tidy, and don't forget to schedule the regular cleaning sessions, lest you be cleaned out.

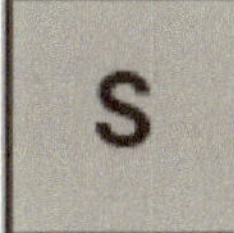

Scheduling

Speaking of scheduling… How can you run a home or a department without that? First, we mean the basics: waking, eating, sleeping. The basic biorhythms, in addition to departing and arriving. If the basics aren't regularised, you have problems.

And this is where you're on your own. This is what you might call a *personal* problem. Even as a professional, this has to do with you *personally.* Run a department without these basics, and you may as well run it straight into the ground.

So, make sure you're setting the right expectations of your personnel and your infrastructure. That they're active for as many hours as they are productive (on the clock, of course), and that they get the rest and refreshment they need to stay that way. In a sense, this too is hygiene, and best dealt with personally.

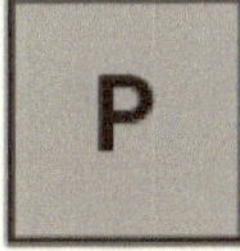

Pause for Face time

Imagine a relationship without face time. And yet, they abound. If you want to know where a relationship is headed, just look at the amount of time—or should we say downtime—a couple give each other. At times it's a meal, other times it's a teatime conversation. And very often, it's a quick chat in the hallway before the day hits you. You've got to make time for this.

And no, tools won't help here. This is a human thing. Make the time for time. And don't just *make* it. Prioritise it. Jot it down in your schedule. Think of the top 3 problems afflicting your department right now, and think of two parties who must assign time to each other to resolve it. It works wonders. And no, we don't mean confrontations. Nor do we mean compromise. We mean collaboration. And, don't stop with problems. Identify opportunities whose value will only be tapped by two minds tapping together. Today it's a business practice, tomorrow it's your competitive advantage.

Pause for Recreation

Recreation? Value? Yes, because "all work and no play makes Jack a dull boy". But we mean this in another sense. We mean if you were to take a little time off and just play about with the tools you have, you never know what you will find. Too few take the time to get to know the tools they're using. Yes, during procurement they compared features, every last one of them, it might seem, and restrict themselves now to using an iota of them.

That is why you must take the time to get "familiar" with the tools that comprise your Martech stack. Familiar, yes—in a familial way—because some value needs to be *teased* out, and how can you tease it out if you wouldn't make time for teasing? Recall that example from earlier, about a data enrichment tool or platform which when added to your website, would greatly elevate your CRM performance. How? That's teasing you, isn't it? So, let's give it to you, since you've taken the time for some winding down time. Ready? Here it is. And if you've never done this before, you'll kick yourself at how easy this was

Let's presume yours is a relatively large organisation, let's say B2B, with a less account-based marketing approach to sales than inbound. Despite your existing customers raving about your product, for some reason, you're still relatively light on the top of your funnel. Why's the bounce rate so high on the form fill page? Well, consider this: a simple tool that extracts and enriches your data set simply from one field—the email ID. Now, if a tool could do that, *would* you need 7 fields in your online form? Of course, not, right? And now you're going to look into this tomorrow morning, aren't you? No? Right away? Go ahead…

Sun and Sand

Still here? Great. Because we want you to hear this: go away. Seriously, go away. Zip off to a haven of sun and sand—or snow, if that's your thing—a hundred miles from the reach of the nearest team outbound. And now that they're all out of earshot, listen close: give your tools a vacation. Send them off on annual vacation, and consider retiring some of them permanently, remembering all the while that it is not the tool or even its features that you're married to. You're married to the value tech can bring.

So when the value shifts from one tech to another, reel it in. And now perhaps you get why we asked you to step away from it all. Because no sooner do your colleagues hear that you're reconsidering your Martech stack, than fear sets in. And fear brings with it all sorts of problems, none of which you want to make yours.

If you're doing this for the first time, there's no better way than to dig your heels in and do it. If you're no first-timer, consider making this a recurring feature, because you want your tools to keep up with your strategy, and not the other way around. Imagine being committed to pivot on a dime, only to discover your Martech stack will be in inertia for 6 months.

Now this isn't to say polyamorous vendor relations are the way to go—loyalty does after all, bring its own value—but it helps to keep them on their toes.

So there you have it. The key to happiness: a 9-step program in eking value from your Martech stack. Is it a coincidence that the letters spell out HAPPINESS, when rearranged? Pure happenstance, if you ask us.

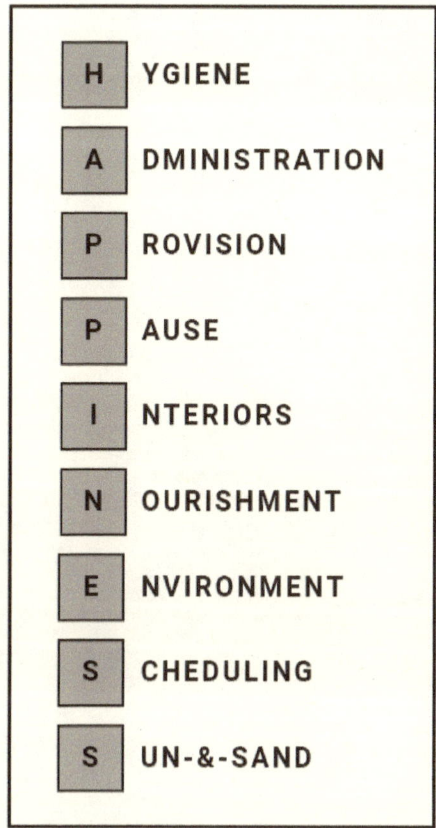

Alright, on to how precisely, you're going to eke the RoI on this relationship.

See you on the next page.

~ ~ ~ ~

Chapter 11

RoI on the Relationship

Before we get into Return on Investment, we must spare a moment on "value". Wait—didn't we just dedicate an entire chapter to it? Yes we did, but hear us out.

The previous chapter had to do with seizing opportunities for value within a team/division/organisation. Oppor*tunities*. But we didn't mention the most valuable thing of all: Opportu*nists*—the Marterchers *doing* the seizing.

And it's important we make that distinction, if we are to truly mine our Marteching™ investments for all they're worth.

So let's begin.

RoI on the Relationship

What are investments? Passive, inanimate and often abstract instruments that do what they are told. They are subject to market fluctuation, and of course, market risk. And that makes *Revenue* on Investment equally so—just outcomes of investments made by inves*tors*. There, we're doing it again: directing your attention to the oft overlooked human element in Marketing. In this case, the inves*tors* behind invest*ment*.

When you're in a relationship, as Martechers are, you realise that these outcomes—RoI—are the result of getting something else right, further upstream. Think about it. Once you have every competitive Martech tool, platform and service out there, and your competition does as well, where's your competitive advantage? First mover? But acceleration can be outpaced by top speed. High barriers to entry? But technology is demolishing those barriers. IP? Now we're getting warmer. But where does intellectual property originate? In the intellect. And who has intellect? People. (AI may mimic intelligence, but that is not the same as intellect.) And you know this to be true, because you can't stand to lose good people. You feel the pain of loss. But switching your Martech tools every now and then? No pain of loss; just the pain of transition. Chaos.

And therefore, relationship. This chapter will present an inverse of RoI. It's called, you guessed it, IoR: Investment on Relationship. This is why, before helping you navigate your Martech stack (we come to that in the next 2 chapters), we spent 4 chapters on People. Opportunists before opportunities.

Let's look at the key Opportunists in Marteching™, and the opportunities they present for value.

To do so, we'll have to combine a few charts from previous chapters. We'll begin with the Design to Delight chart from the Silos chapter and expand on it over the next few pages.

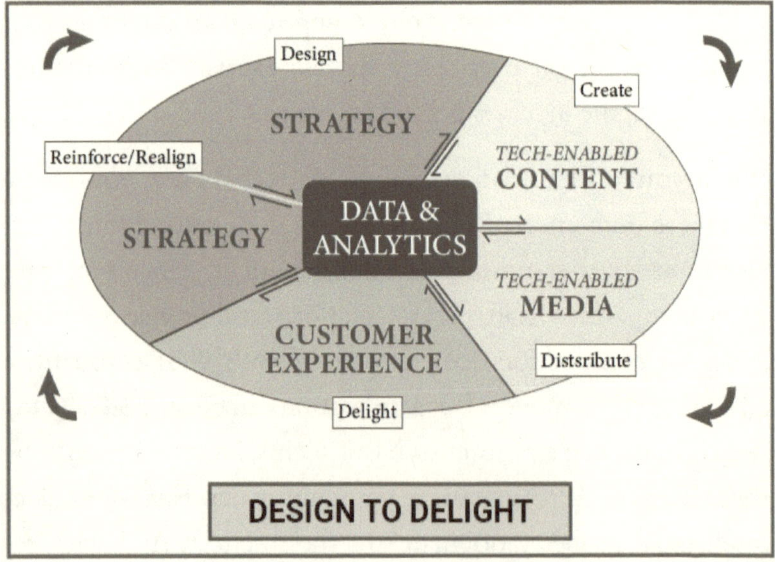

This chart represents more or less the flow of value creation in Marketing as well as digital-led Advertising. However, when they look at this chart, Marketers and their Ad agencies see very different things, despite often having the same capabilities. And this is why Adtech and Martech are such different businesses, Adtech limiting itself to delivering advertising experiences, and Martech broadening its scope further upstream *and* downstream from there.

What we want to do in this chapter is take you through a single Marteching™ experience all the way across the value cycle. From Strategy through Content, Media, CX and back, with Data egging us all along the way.

To do that, we must first give you an overview of the teams and lead roles you're likely to encounter in a Marteching™ environment, which will give you a great lay of the land. As we proceed, you may see familiar roles being described in unfamiliar ways. That's because the same marketing role performs very differently in a B2B vs a B2C environment, with differences being noted even industry to industry. For instance, a digital marketer working in a typically long-cycle, account-based B2B sales approach will be expected to work with the firm's Customer Relationship Management (CRM) tool, whereas the same digital marketer operating in a retail environment will see themselves working in far shorter cycles, even going so far as to work with the firm's e-commerce platform.

We will begin with a general "forest" view and then the more granular "tree" view, without going so close as to point out the bark and the leaves.

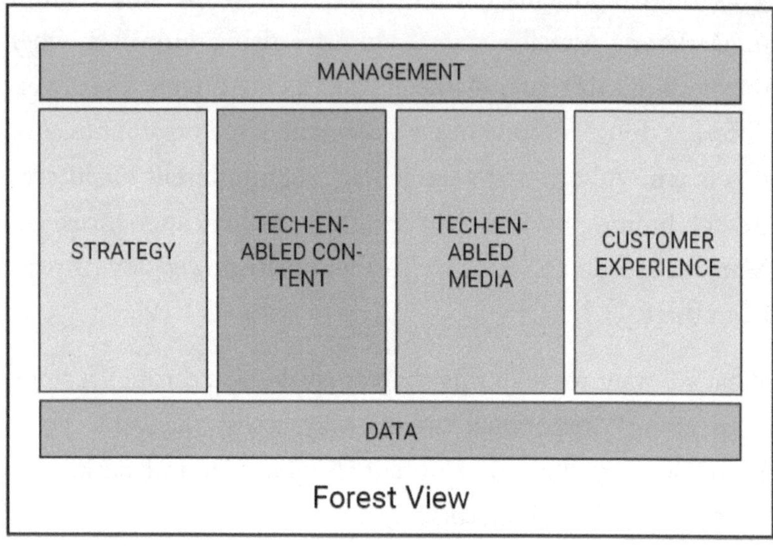

First, a view of the Forest: Management, Data and Everything in Between

MANAGEMENT

What is Management managing? When taking a top view, you see the advertising and marketing process typically begin with Strategy, moving on to Content—both visual and verbal—then Media, and eventually the Customer Experience, with Data boomeranging in and out, adding value every step of the way, and feeding the insights and analytics back into Strategy, enhancing the overall process. Take a look at the People-Process-Practice chart introduced in Chapter 3. Well, when Management brings in the right People, they are able to work towards improving the discipline in Process, leading to the perfect Marteching™ Practice.

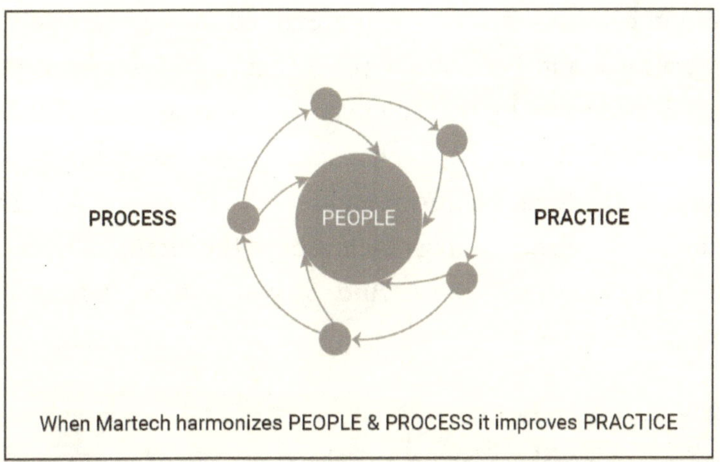

When Martech harmonizes PEOPLE & PROCESS it improves PRACTICE

DATA

Although Marteching™ data has to do with People, it is impersonal. The tool may analyse, but the human interprets. At every stage in the process, the Data core relays information to and fro. It is designed to do so by a mix of skills: Data Scientists, Stewards, Analysts and so on. And here, those in Data need to remember that their discipline is at the core simply because that is where your Customer is. Conversely, if Data isn't at your core, that's because your customer isn't. Marketing that is customer-centric can't *but* have Data at its core. Of course, this puts the pressure to perform squarely on Data's shoulders, but as we will see, there are other able-minded professionals around, to help bring that about.

EVERYTHING IN BETWEEN

Strategy

Despite Data being at the core, everything begins (and ends) with Strategy. Strategy takes place at two times, and here we don't mean the way it is represented in the chart—that's Operations, and we will come to that. Strategy at the very start is originated by Management. It is Management that lays out its needs of the Martech stack, designs accordingly, and brings in the tools, platforms and services necessary. With that blueprint in place, Strategy then proceeds operationally in the project management sense. And, as you've seen, it starts *and* ends the process.

Content

Content is, purely speaking, the visual and verbal manifestation of Strategy, brought about with pixels and bits and bytes, and, even in this digital age, ink on your advertising medium of choice. Content is developed by two different disciplines of writer and designer who together turn the Strategy into assets aimed at a human reaction: interest, engagement, purchase, recommendation, that sort of thing. This is why you need the *least* technical and most 'human' personnel working in Content. They're creating for a sea of indifference out there. Unless someone opts into an experience, most brand communication is an interruption. This makes the Content team's job two-fold: (1) create demand and (2) fulfil demand. All too often the Content department is oriented around fulfilling the demand already created by other Media such as Television or Influencer Marketing.

Media

Media. What an all encompassing word, like "value". Unfortunately, we can't even narrow it down, in today's day of media explosion and fragmentation. Nevertheless, for those fragments to turn into shrapnel, we need the discipline of Media Planning. And we don't mean the typical Media Planning operation that takes place at the start of a marketing campaign—that's Operations. We mean planning the Media choices at our disposal, assigning each to a leg in the journey, one most suited to the typical attribution associated with it. If that sounded like a mouthful, take this simple example: say you're an FMCG brand, with, for argument's sake, 3 Media at your disposal: Search, Display and OOH (out-of-home). What's your expectation of OOH? Demand Creation. And Search? Demand Fulfilment. Display? Well, depending on your product and the reach of your brand, and where you are in the campaign, somewhere in between. This thinking also influences how you design your Martech stack, which we touch on briefly in Chapter 13.

Customer Experience

Germany's flag carrier Lufthansa launched a classic ad campaign decades ago titled "All for this one moment". And that is truly what Customer Experience (aka CX) is: the alchemy of every Marketing decision and component in the Martech stack, all for "that one moment". What does all the world's greatest Strategy, Content, Media and Data—not to mention Management—matter if your Marteching™ effort fails at the CX level? CX is where 2 kinds of actions take place: one, the customer is prompted to take an action—engage or ignore? And two, your Data core extracts these user events, analyses and distributes them to Content and Media for tactical interventions, and back to Strategy for deeper interpretation and prescription. (See why Data's at the core? Because the customer is.)

Now, for the "Tree" view.

Disclaimer: Given how rapidly roles and responsibilities shift as the demand around them shifts, we took the wisest course, and amalgamated them all under their respective managerial function. That way, you will navigate through a classic value-driven structure without getting caught up in the minutiae.

STRATEGY MANAGEMENT

Marketing Director

Let's begin at the very top. What is a Marketing Director responsible for? In short, everything. But let us elaborate. Think of the 4 Ps: Product, Price, Place, Promotion. Whose domain is that? That of the head of Marketing. They're the meeting point of every discipline that answers to Marketing, which makes them as much generalists as they are expected to be specialists. A Marketing Director's particular specialisation/s will determine the orientation and culture of a Marketing department.

Marketing Technologist

If you're thinking—wait, isn't that the one responsible for evaluating and implementing Martech at our organisation? The one responsible for managing data and technology integration and ensuring our Martech is aligned with business objectives? And that the Marketing team has what they need to deliver on these objectives? You're right, and that saved us all the trouble of having to explain it. The job of a Marketing Technologist also involves a bit of research—they're definitely the SMEs (Subject Matter Experts) on all things Martech. They're where the buck stops. And since they're the SPOC (Single Point of Contact) in vendor evaluation and procurement, they're also where the buck starts. Martech being an emerging field, most Martech professionals are still somewhere early on the learning curve, which makes it the Marketing Technologist's job to not just architect the Martech stack, but also act as an evangelist of Martech, upskilling people and designing processes. If there is a proliferation of composable architecture in your Martech, be it for composable DXPs, low-code app builders or no-code databases, it's because your Marketing Director and Marketing Technologist talk, or they're the same person.

Digital Marketing Manager

Here's one title where you will certainly recognise multiple roles. In the interest of brevity and sanity of mind, we will lump them all under a "Digital Marketing Manager" role, while being careful not to stray too far into the Media Manager's territory, as happens all too often at the workplace. A management role in Digital Marketing would include creating the digital marketing strategy, developing full-funnel campaigns across media assets leveraging every conceivable customer touchpoint, optimising search, monitoring trends, directing traffic, routing digital analytics and even business intelligence through to respective teams, managing affiliate marketing and at times even affiliates, in short, everything. Did we miss anything? Oh yeah, "Performance Marketing", whatever that means, as if to make the inference of such a thing as non-performance Marketing.

DATA MANAGEMENT

Data Scientist

Before Data Scientists came along, we were already creating data taxonomies, building content models and working LoopBack models. But not quite the same way. Data Scientists working in the age of AI and Machine Learning (ML) have taken analytics to the next level: from predictive to prescriptive. And when working in Martech, they don't restrict themselves to activities like clustering, anomaly detection, neural networks and post-deployment validation. Marketing being oriented around the customer has brought in many softer aspects to Data Science, such as the power of observation, the delicacy of nuance or just being able to see behavioural economics actually at work. And then, comes the joy of building something that's never been built before. Feature Engineering.Time Series Forecasting. And if there's a Data Scientist reading this with a wry smile, we'll leave a blank space here for your current pet project ____________.

Data Steward

If the Data Scientist is the architect, the Data Steward is the interior designer. And that's a great comparison, because they make the best use of the available features or constraints just the way interior designers do. Of course, it sounds nothing like what interior designers do: extracting, transforming and loading data from multiple sources to a data warehouse or lake; migrating data across systems and protocols; ensuring data are accurate, accessible and secure; mastering everything from data lineage to data linkage. Not to mention developing data standards, rules and quality metrics for various data sets if the job calls for it. It's all in a day's work for a Data Steward. You may never actually come across one—at least not one with that description—in the hallways of Martech, but their presence is felt nevertheless.

Analytics Manager

Depending on the organisation you work at, the previous two roles would operate out of the DevOps or DataOps function. If your data systems contain homegrown design or architecture, it's very probable that they had something to do with it. Let's introduce a more familiar face: the Analytics Manager. What does he manage? Well, everything involving customer data actions and data-driven business decisions. And what a spectrum of tasks that is, beginning with defining the appropriate analytics frameworks, tools and processes at one end, and automating every predictable and repetitive task at the other. While in the middle, making time to identify and build the right set of vendors and partners, pair business-critical analytics inputs with rock-solid outputs (think visualisations the teams can use), democratising data access across Marketing and even beyond, and, every Martecher's dream, providing Management with weighted attributions to how their Marketing's doing at every digital touchpoint, be it a cross-sectional view (moment in a campaign) or longitudinal (duration of a campaign).Did we hear a "They can do what?" Oh yeah, they can.

CONTENT MANAGEMENT

Campaign Planner

First, there's no such thing as a Campaign Planner, it's just a container title for what's actually an extremely broad job title that differs across industries, and even *within* organisations. That is because the word "campaign" itself means so many different things in different business contexts. To simplify this, there is the Hero-Hub-Hygiene model, which plots the kind of campaign you're dealing with by size and significance.

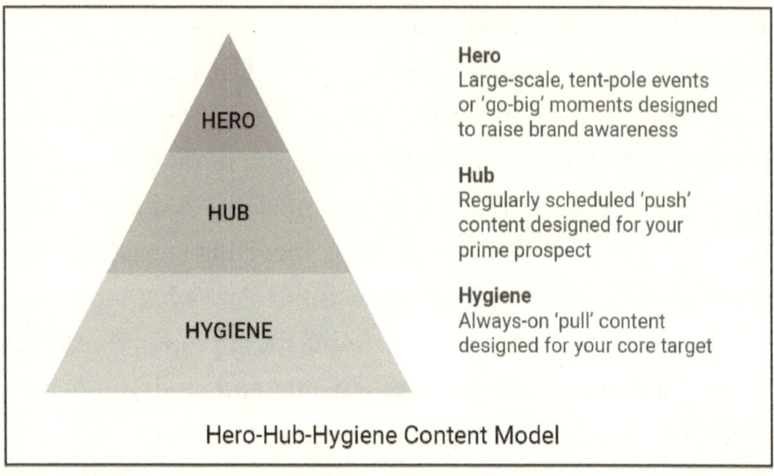

Hero-Hub-Hygiene Content Model

To a big-budget Marketer, "campaign" = big-budget integrated marketing communication involving at least a few touchpoints. That's generally a Hero campaign, done sparingly during the year. This very same Marketer may also engage in Hub campaigns from time to time, bringing in the seasonal spikes which inject growth into a brand's sales and awareness metrics. To a Marketer with a smaller budget, Hubs are Heroes, and that's all they've ever known. The third category, Hygiene, is generally common across Marketers. It means being mentally and physically present in season and out of season: being easy to recall, easy to find, and easy to buy.

When most Martechers say "campaign", they generally mean something of the Hygiene or Hub kind. This is because at present Martech is seen from the outside as a "stack" of tools that stand to optimise or fine-tune the digital aspects of going to market. But that's just techwashing: putting up an appearance of prioritising tech in Marketing, while failing to see its true transformative potential.

So given this context, what does Campaign Planning involve? It first means turning the expectations businesses may have of their product/service into a campaign brief which instructs and challenges the various Content stakeholders to develop a campaign that addresses or exceeds the business needs. We will expand on this in the next chapter.

MEDIA MANAGEMENT

Media Planner

First, yes, this role exists in Marteching™. But, not the way traditional Marketers may be familiar with, where the Media Planner strategises over the optimum media mix and media spend for a brand campaign—something Hero or Hub. That isn't to say the Marteching™ Media Planner doesn't work on Hero campaigns, but that theirs is a specialist role, more to do with orchestrating and optimising brand outcomes within digital ecosystems. This is where, lamentably, many Media Planners fall behind, when the Adtech they work with lags behind where Martech is today. If you were to beam yourself from a Media Planner's desk in Advertising to their counterpart in Marketing, you would scarcely believe they share the same title. But well, that's what tools can do, and with Adtech lagging behind the way it is, it's a matter of time before Advertising Media Planners either shift to the Martech mindset or get left behind.

CX MANAGEMENT

Customer Experience Manager

You may work in a Marteching™ environment that has never hired a CX Manager. Nevertheless, you will find their roles and responsibilities scattered across various teams in your organisation, such as someone in Strategy, Content or UX (user experience). The CX Manager brings in value in quite a few interesting ways: modelling data-based customer journeys, validating and implementing research findings, turning user insights into marketable customer personas, or *usage* insights into frictionless customer experiences.

Product Manager (UX)

Similar to a Customer Experience Manager, a Product Manager is a champion of the Customer Experience, and as much a VoC (voice of the customer) as a CX counterpart. The key difference is the Product Manager exerts a certain technical prowess over that experience, being able to deliver on customer needs and expectations through UX itself. Those in this role are generally expected to demonstrate design leadership, which includes drafting of the UX vision for a tool or team, developing a UI/UX roadmap, establishing benchmarks, and so on.

And now, the moment you've all been waiting for: watching that ONE Marteching™ experience zip through all the way from Strategy through Content, Media, CX and back. But first, let's talk football.

~ ~ ~ ~

Chapter 12

Total Marteching™

About 50 years ago, back when Diego Maradona was still playing the junior division, the Dutch nation saw a phenomenon. Its football team, with no superstars to speak of, started winning everywhere. And nobody could put a stop to it.

The juggernaut came to be known as Total Football (the Spaniards call it tiki-taka). Its poster boy Johan Cruyff, described it as a strategy where anyone (barring the goalkeeper) could play anywhere. It was the perfect combination of player movement, coordination, and spacing. And it worked. For too long the Italians' defensive "catenaccio" dominated the field, scoring a goal, only to then fall back to their defensive positions, and keep the offense out. But they couldn't keep the Dutch out.

The Dutch would pass, probe, pass again, probe some more, and keep working the ball until an opportunity presented itself, and then BAM. A goal from out of nowhere. They were opportu*nists* of the highest caliber.

And that's the perfect segue into the world of business, where truly gifted opportunists patiently carve out opportunities amidst the thrill of high stakes, evenly-matched opponents, roaring fans on either side, and at the close of day's play, a winner and a loser.

We closed the last chapter off with a hint: we were going to show you how to string every conceivable value opportunity together into a single, unified view owned by Marketing.

And, here it is.

It starts with a word we've almost forgotten today: brief.

A brief is the strategic starting point in marketing communication. Its disuse is especially tragic when you realise it is *part* of strategy, which is the starting point of *marketing*.

To return Marketing once more to its former "seat at the table", Martechers must return to Marketing's roots, and apply the promise of Tech to the precise opportunities where it will yield results. Where it has *always* yielded results

This chapter will explore these opportunities from two angles: from the perspective of Marketing strategy and from Communication strategy. As we open up the playbook you will find yourself on familiar territory. You will notice some dos and some don'ts. You will see cringe-worthy plays, and the commendable, just as with any sport.

The referee whistles, the crowd roars, and we're off.

The opponent drives the ball deep into your team's territory, but are nabbed at the last moment by the striker, a Copywriter. 90 yards away he espies the goal, and darts off. Let's see what happens next.

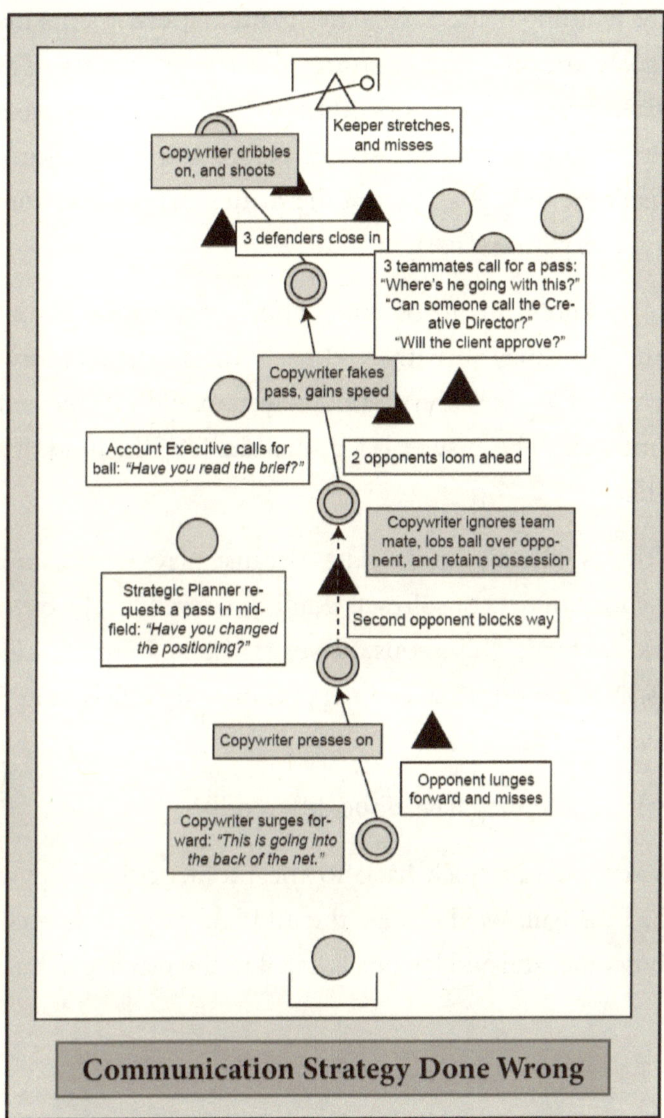

Communication Strategy Done Wrong

The crowd erupts. It's what they paid for.

But is a goal all there is to sport?

Surely, winning matters. Matches matter. Tournaments matter. But goals are only one measure of a team's success. There's practice, psyche, teamwork... In football as in business, so much goes on behind the scenes before going live. Scoring a goal isn't the only goal. Fact of the matter is, it's an outcome of getting everything else right.

And you know this to be true. Think back to the n number of times you may've witnessed such a moment in sport, and ask yourself if those very same players could've repeated the performance. The answer is a dismal shake of the head. It's not very likely.

And this is why playbooks exist. Because plays take teamwork. One-shot wonders or solo acts don't do so well for the business. Think of change in seasons, player transfers, injuries, and low spells. No, no business can depend on individuals, any more than a sport can.

So, what could they have done differently?

Let's rewind the clock back to the moment the Copywriter nabbed the ball. We'll change the midfield play, while retaining the outcome, and add lessons learned to the playbook's margin.

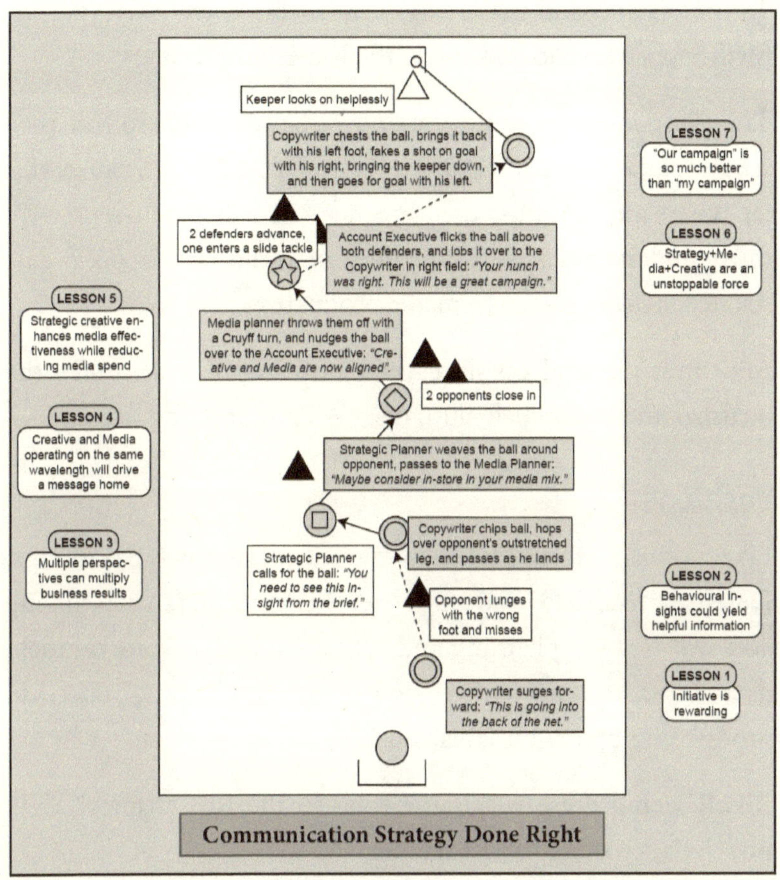

Communication Strategy Done Right

The crowd erupts. It's more than what they paid for.

Is the outcome the same? Both plays ended with a goal, but in the latter, the team achieved much more than a goal. They gained insight, increased in perspective, honed their instinct, outwitted their opponent, and had so much more to celebrate at the end of it than just a solo artist's skill.

And what kept them united? You said it: the brief.

To understand and master the unified brief, we must journey further upstream to its source: the Marketing strategy.

The components of strategy are now a familiar sight to you: they are People, Process and Practice. When speaking of Strategy this far upstream, we must use "Practice" in a different sense. We must understand it as a container of multiple practices: data science, market research, media production, and so on.

And now, we find ourselves in a boardroom (not unlike the boardroom at a football club) discussing Marketing strategy.

Positions

Like football, business too is comprised of essentially 3 positions: Defense, Midfield and Offense. In your defensive lineup you will include planning and strategy roles, in your midfield data and operations and in your offense everything related to production: content, media and CX.

Recall seeing these very same roles in the RoI chapter? Well, now let's see them work together.

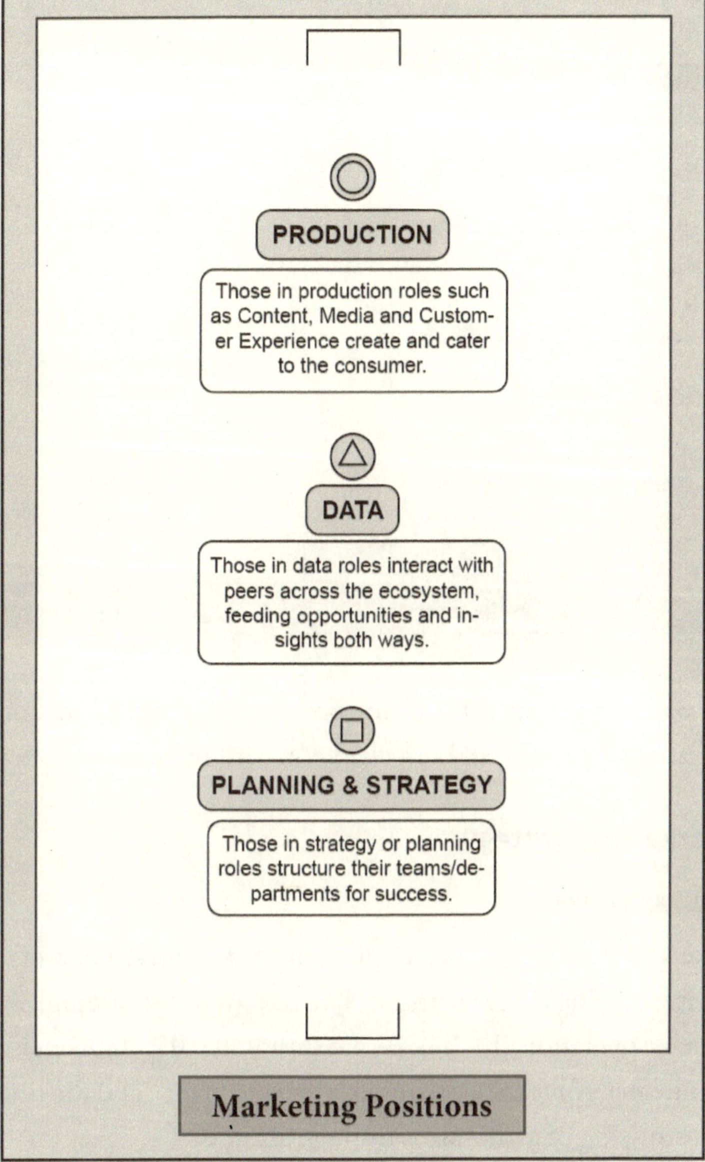
PRODUCTION
Those in production roles such as Content, Media and Customer Experience create and cater to the consumer.
DATA
Those in data roles interact with peers across the ecosystem, feeding opportunities and insights both ways.
PLANNING & STRATEGY
Those in strategy or planning roles structure their teams/departments for success.
Marketing Positions

Formations

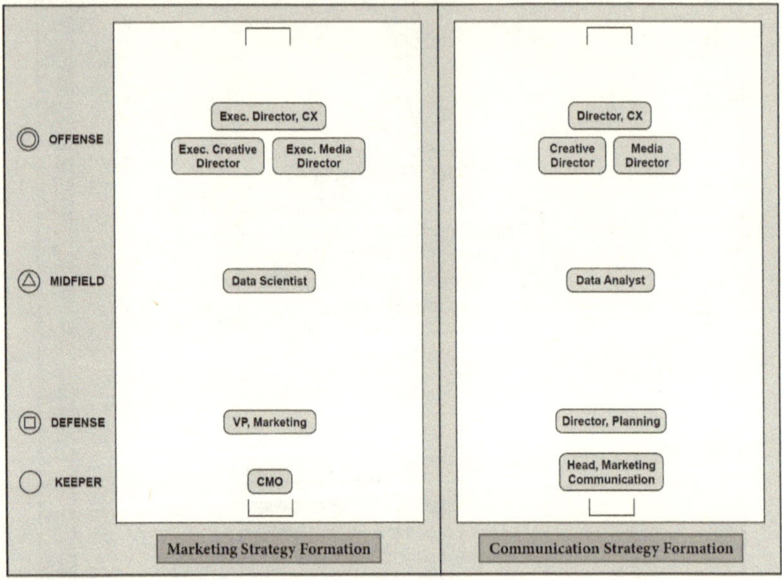

Marketing Strategy Formation

Communication Strategy Formation

As with any competitive team sport, the ultimate formation is a matter of strategy, and can change according to the situation.

Marketing Strategy

CMO as Keeper

Like the goalkeeper, the CMO enjoys a central view of the entire playing field without having to move around very much, operationally. Their proximity to the thinkers and planners permits the occasion of strategic pivots, and the timely transmission of game-plans during runtime.

VP, Marketing, as Defense

This is the CMO's feet on street, and ears on ground. Being occupied in Marketing Operations, the VP is best suited to assist in the structuring of a Marteching™ department, *and* extending that vision to every day operations around meeting the brief.

Data Scientist as Midfield

Placed in this position, the Data employee is most effective, and most dangerous. Their insights and opportunities are fed bi-directionally, frustrating and drawing out the opposition. You lose midfield, you lose the game.

Production Executives as Offense

Strikers traditionally occupy their opposition's territory. But in Total Football, they're everywhere. And that is what makes them deadly. What does this mean for your department? Cross-functional exposure. Give your Creative, Media and CX professionals a panoramic view of your Martech suite, and invite opportunities for creative intervention.

Communication Strategy

Head, Marketing Communication, as Keeper

The VP is an ambidextrous marketer, crafting strategy with one hand, and orchestrating it with the other. Just like a keeper. If you're looking for *one* role that works end-to-end marketing from strategy to brief and back, this is the one.

Director, Planning, as Defense

When delivering on a brief, the Planning Director is the impenetrable force that keeps chaos and incoherence at bay.

What's more, they're the ones uniquely positioned and skilled enough to deal with Data coming in from Midfield, and long back passes from Offense that compel them to launch counter-strategies on the go.

Data Analyst as Midfield

At the end of day's play, the stats read win/lose, with goals being the defining factor. Few people dig deeper to acknowledge, let alone commend the dedication of the midfield, creating and sensing opportunities, relaying information forward and back, testing and trying the opposition... Today, with data analysis and interpretation, those days are finally numbered.

Production Executives as Offense

Everybody enjoys a great ad, or product experience. For that, we have the finesse of the strikers to thank. After all, if they don't strike gold, all is lost. But in today's day and age, they can't afford to silo as specialists; they've *got* to get around the field, putting themselves in ever new and challenging positions, for the sake of the end goal: and that is winning.

⋆ ⋆ ⋆

Choose your formation

As CMO, you know your strengths and weaknesses best, and that of your competition. So go ahead and choose the formation that works best for you. Does your team currently have missing roles to fill? Which are your weakest spots? What skill trainings does your squad currently need? Address these gaps as you create your winning squad. And above all, create and own that single artefact which drives it all: the unified brief.

We've spoken about the unified brief. But what *is* it? What does it look like? Let's begin with Strategy. Let's say you're a B2B manufacturing firm with a global presence. We're in the boardroom, and a decision is being taken. A decision that involves financing a new sales enablement platform. It's expensive (says the CFO), but potentially lucrative (says your report), and now all eyes are on the Chief Sales Officer: is the reward worth the risk? Depending on your organisation's culture and the grit of its key personnel, this decision could go either way. They break for lunch, during which time you approach a few key players, and airdrop certain trivia (custom to their role) which you know will pique interest. Post lunch the decision is more or less taken, and it's a win for you. Despite this product being owned by the Sales team, you had championed it from the wings for two reasons: first, its attribution logic was virtually flawless. Finally, you thought, Finance will be able to actually see the RoI on our Marketing activities. And second, the product seemed to share your vision for a more unified Sales+Marketing approach to business wins.

The weeks roll by, the platform has onboarded both Sales and Marketing, and things are moving swimmingly.

Now, imagine this. You have a big campaign coming up, and as you build it, it becomes painfully aware that the Marketing team don't see the convergence of Sales+Marketing as you do. It hasn't even occurred to them.

Now you're 3 weeks from going live, and you can see more pressing pain points than there are hours in the day. But despite it all, you know the *one* thing that will solve the majority of your problems: a sit-down with your key personnel.

You ask them to present their strategy which you've seen before, and at the first weak point, you step in and offer your analysis: this approach won't work for us anymore, since Sales and Marketing are converging.

The words hang heavy. Weren't we discussing the campaign? What's this high-level talk? And that is when you present this chart. Remember it from the chapter on Silos?

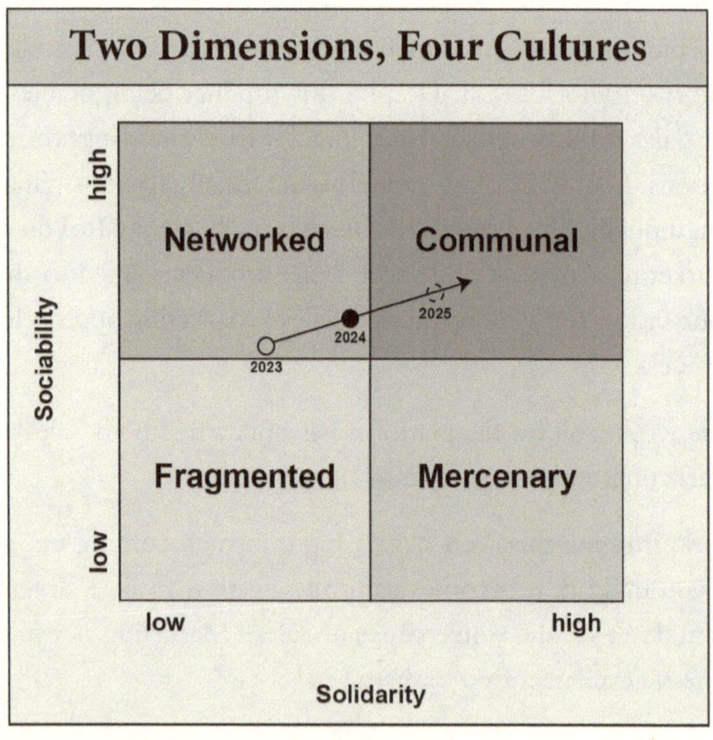

On it we will plot 3 points: where we want Sales-Marketing collaboration to be in 2025, the current moment in time, and where we were when we first charted this course. Then, we will draw a vector between the 3, signifying this moment in time, and the sales-marketing collaboration being discussed.

You sense these questions in the air, and continue: it's been 2 months since Sales was onboarded onto the enablement platform, and so far they've had only good things to say. In short, the time is now ripe for Sales and Marketing to tangibly work together, and this campaign presents an immense opportunity to test the waters.

Glances are exchanged. Your deputies are not sure what to make of this. You assure them that you have the CSO's buy-in, and that casting their anxieties aside they will learn much, and in coming together, sharpen their competitive advantage in the market. You remind a few of them how their KPIs are linked to sales outcomes, and that closer collaboration will benefit all.

That does the trick, and later in the week, you've had your first Sales+Marketing kickoff for the campaign, and, things once more, are proceeding swimmingly.

If we were to plot your rather unorthodox team formation on the playing field, we'd probably see something like this.

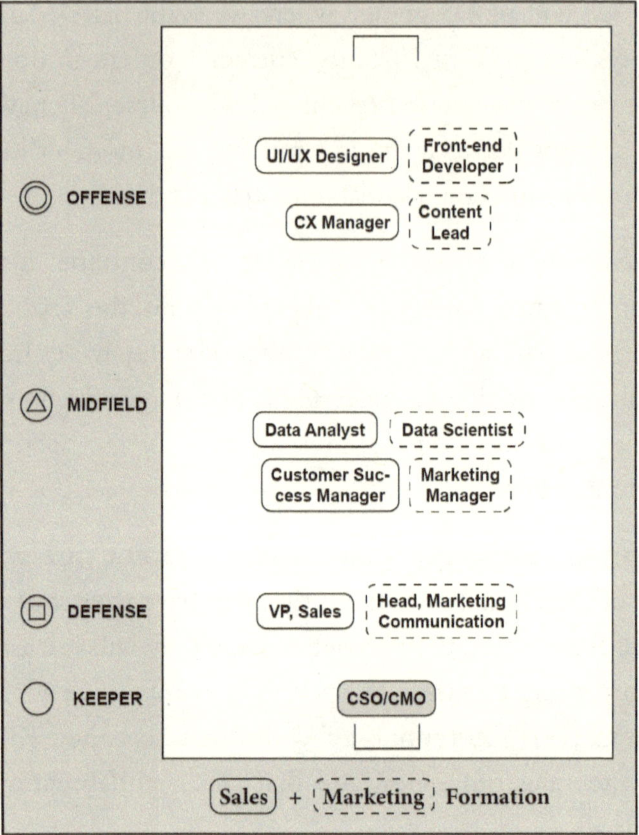

How's that for breaking down silos, and investing on Relationship?

And the best part is this. In the above scenario, your Marketing Brief was based on your high-level Marketing Strategy.

So let's recap what we've learned so far:

1) Like Total Football, Total Marteching™ is marked by player movement, coordination and spacing
2) This is facilitated at the workplace by a single unified view bringing strategy and briefs into alignment

3) Both artefacts (briefs and strategy) are best owned by Marketing
4) Team positions are fixed, but team formations are fluid

Now that we've cleared the air on strategy and the brief, and the need for an unobstructed passage between the two, let's roll out a single scenario from end to end.

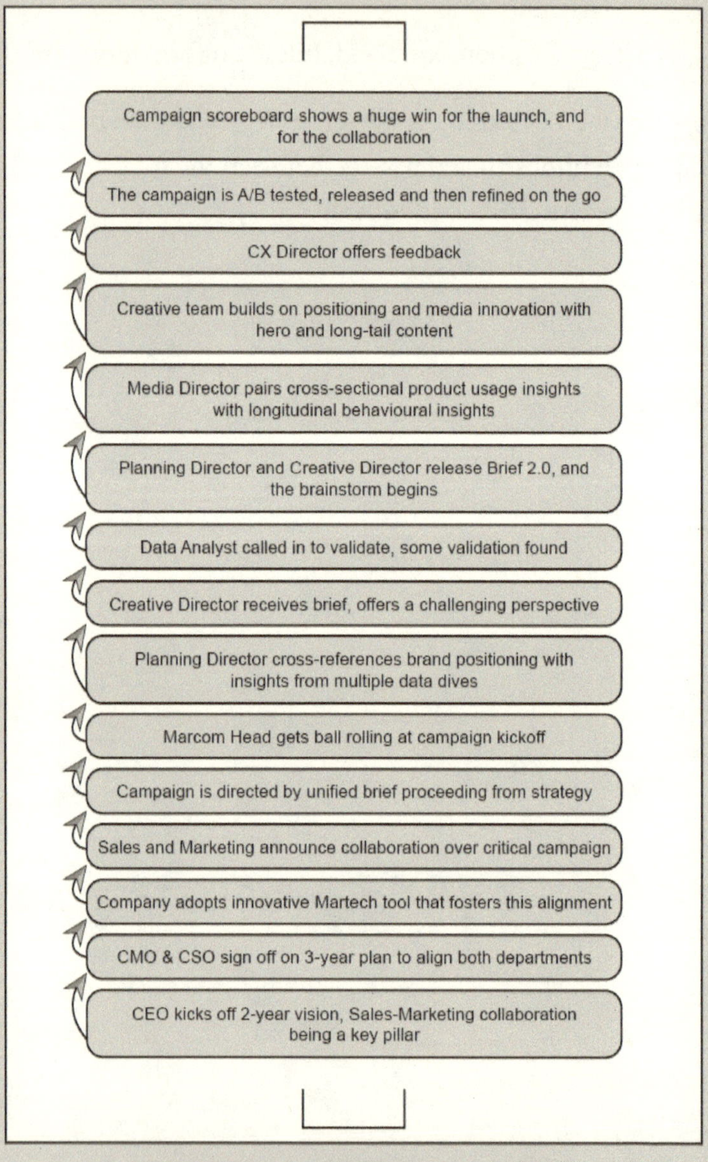

Campaign scoreboard shows a huge win for the launch, and for the collaboration

The campaign is A/B tested, released and then refined on the go

CX Director offers feedback

Creative team builds on positioning and media innovation with hero and long-tail content

Media Director pairs cross-sectional product usage insights with longitudinal behavioural insights

Planning Director and Creative Director release Brief 2.0, and the brainstorm begins

Data Analyst called in to validate, some validation found

Creative Director receives brief, offers a challenging perspective

Planning Director cross-references brand positioning with insights from multiple data dives

Marcom Head gets ball rolling at campaign kickoff

Campaign is directed by unified brief proceeding from strategy

Sales and Marketing announce collaboration over critical campaign

Company adopts innovative Martech tool that fosters this alignment

CMO & CSO sign off on 3-year plan to align both departments

CEO kicks off 2-year vision, Sales-Marketing collaboration being a key pillar

Marteching™ Done Right

There you have it. With just the right amount of player movement, coordination and spacing, two often competing departments can come together to achieve common goals when they work on a single unified briefing method owned by Marteching™.

~ ~ ~ ~

Chapter 13

Martech to Experience Tech

In the last chapter, we showed you how player movement, coordination and spacing can bring competing departments together to achieve common goals.

The manner in which they achieve this is what we called Total Marteching™, and the means by which they do so is the single unified brief owned by the Marteching™ department.

This chapter will take you higher; above the playing field and into the stands, where the customer is seated on edge, awaiting the next high. Let us examine how we Martechers can better see, serve and surprise this audience.

SEE

What the fans see is very different from what the players, coaches or managers see. They brim with excitement at a promising play, and erupt when a goal is scored or saved.

Think of a brand like Spotify, who release several highlights during the year, the most awaited being "Wrapped", where they present each user with a unique dashboard of their Spotify account, replete with insights, trivia and other truly personalised data that's worth the wait.

But do their users see the global scale of such a project? Would its immense complexity and meticulous planning cross their minds, while they browse through "2023 Wrapped"? Hardly. And yet, that is what it takes.

To the players, coaches and managers—and now let's place ourselves in the Marteching™ department—their omnichannel marketing strategy has more than its share of challenges and opportunities. You know this. If you were to close your eyes right now and only imagine the various touchpoints a single customer has to engage with your brand, it might take you a minute or two to go over them all.

But the customer doesn't see you that way. To the customer in the stands or watching via satellite, you are 11 players on a field, negotiating with 11 others as you move a ball about towards the high point they've paid to see, which is a well-earned goal or save at either end of the playing area.

Switching the view from being on the field to being in the stands is not easy. Think of global stars like Lionel Messi and Cristiano Ronaldo who've struggled to play this birds eye view mode of the beautiful game on a console.

But switch we must, if we are to be true Marketers in the era of Marteching™.

Let's start by looking at 5 basic touchpoints:

- Convey
- Compare
- Commit
- Care
- Convey

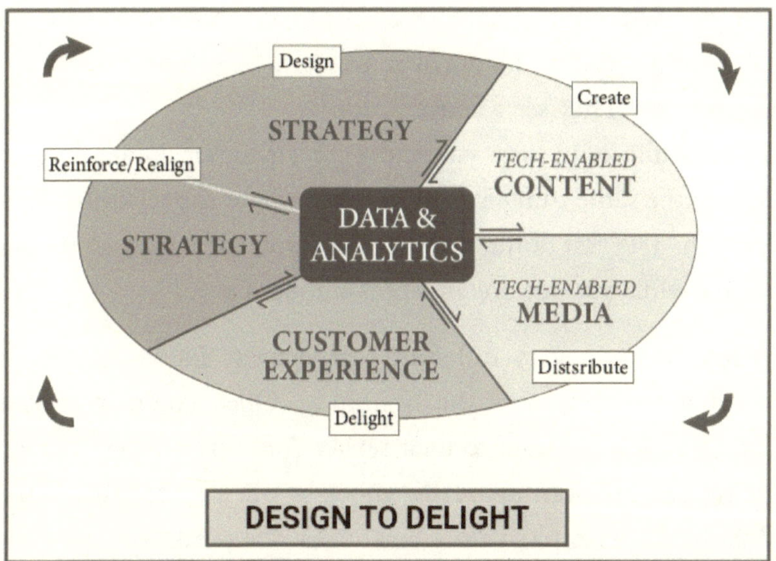

We will examine what you see vs what your customer or prospect sees, all across the funnel.

- When you **CONVEY** your brand message on a single touchpoint
  - o You see one touchpoint among many
  - o They see one brand among many
- When they **COMPARE** your brand v/s others
  - o You see one lead entering your data set
  - o They see one brand entering their consideration set
- When they **COMMIT** by purchasing your brand
  - o You see customer lifetime value
  - o They see value in your offering
- When they solicit your **CARE** in after-sales
  - o You see an opportunity to deepen the relationship
  - o They see an opportunity to prove the relationship

- When they **CONVEY** your brand above others
    - o You see potential conversion
    - o They see a conversation

Perhaps the only time you and your customer come close to seeing the same thing is in after-sales, where the relationship is proven. The rest of the time, they see you as one brand among many, while you see one prospect among many.

These are two very different perspectives. However, seeing what they see is only the beginning. Once you're past that gate, you have to cater to their reality. And this is where brands acing the relationship really knock it out of the park. Take Netflix for example, whose personalised algorithm keeps their customers coming back. The customer sees a dashboard rich with entertainment, but Netflix sees a dashboard rich with data. How do they do it? They don't say. But the customers don't care. They just keep coming back for more, and Netflix is ready when they are.

How do they balance our desire for freshness with our need for familiarity? Beats us: you'd have to ask Netflix.

SERVE

Now that you can see what they see, you can serve from *their* perspective, not yours. And, what's more, you can optimise your supply end, to weed out practices that add complexity to the demand end while blunting your competitive edge.

Beginning in 2017, Home Depot did exactly that. They began serving their customers' needs first, by portraying their product offering from *their* perspective. So, rather than seeing the store arranged by *product* category, the customers saw it arranged by *project* category. Which suited them just fine, because that is how *they* saw Home Depot. While Home Depot saw themselves as the home improvement retailer with *everything* "home improvement" on offer, their customers were more specific in their requirement, and therefore, how *they* saw Home Depot. They began to think of Home Depot only after having carved out a home improvement project or stage, such as plumbing, or painting. And depending on which one came first, if Home Depot snapped the prospect up then, they were more likely to continue coming back for future stages of home improvement.

Here's how that CX initiative might've burrowed its way into and through the organisation, beginning with customer feedback, and ending with a retail innovation.

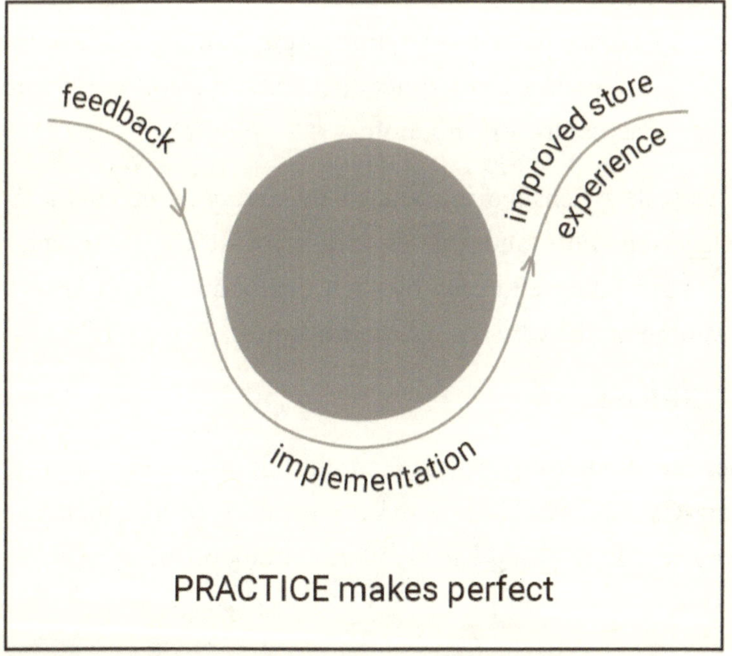

Now how's THAT for home improvement?

But here's where it gets interesting. For Home Depot to improve its retail experience, it would need to introduce corresponding improvements in every department contributing to that experience.

That would mean improving:

- MERCHANDISING
  A complete store layout overhaul allowing customers to discover and purchase all items related to their project in one place, rather than across the store
- INTERFACES
  Intuitive digital interfaces and trained human staff offering timely information, guidance and assistance
- OPERATIONS
  Logistics, redesign, refurbishing, training and execution of such a cross-functional initiative combines forces across the organisation

The scale of change introduced by that *one* improvement is staggering, but—and this is important—carried through to the exhilarating end only by such organisations that keep the customer at the very core of their business.

SURPRISE

Service is one thing, surprise another. If you've ever been to a Ritz-Carlton, you'll know what we mean. (And, you'll know why you keep going back.) What is it about the Ritz, that no matter how hard their competitors try, they can never imitate them?

If you've ever been to a Ritz twice, you'll remember the first time they surprised you. Maybe it was the contents of your minibar. "How'd *they* know I was thinking about salted cashew nuts?" Or the arrangement of your toiletries. Déjà vu. Maybe it's a fruit you enjoyed in one country, but were surprised to see in another, that too off season.

The world of CX is replete with such stories of one-off cases where a brand went overboard to delight a customer. The trick is not just repeating the performance, but making it a part of your process, and then practice.

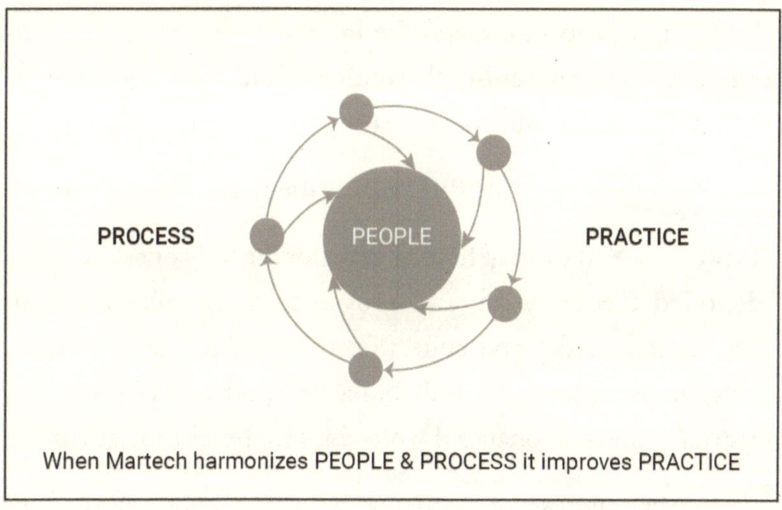

When Martech harmonizes PEOPLE & PROCESS it improves PRACTICE

The good news is that all of the above—seeing, serving and surprising your customers—are more than ably aided in the age of Martech.

Say you were thinking about a morning coffee. (Now I didn't say Starbucks, but chances are that would've wormed its way into your mind even quicker than I could say the word.) And let's say the thought of coffee struck you at a not very opportune time—you were *just* about to leave for work. What do you do?

Stop right there, and mentally file this away as the Customer's challenge.

Now, imagine you're a coffee shop (no doubt you're thinking Starbucks, again), well aware of the morning habits of your clientele. For every 10 morning coffees you hand out, you notice 7 are not so much received as grabbed. 9, on a Monday morning. There's an insight there: our morning customers are in a hurry. But there's more. You also note the amount of rush there is most mornings, and the link between standing-room-only and the grab-and-dash routine. Could we decrease the rush while maintaining or increasing the payout?

Stop right there, and file this away as the Brand's opportunity.

If you can see an overlap here, you're not the only one. Starbucks identified this early on, and provided an app allowing their customers to order and collect on the go. And, with a virtual merchandising logic not unlike that of Spotify or Netflix, they customise and personalise the offerings for best business results.

All in the interest of reducing mental friction. And that's something Martech stands to do so well. If you've been seeing Martech as the Marketing equivalent of Sales enablement, that statement sticks out, doesn't it? How could Martech reduce a customer's mental friction? Think of a stationary bike or treadmill. One with an inbuilt screen connecting you to the best instructors and regimens, customised to your fitness level and appetite. You're thinking of Peloton, aren't you? How did you do that? Because there is little mental friction between the brand and its attribute. Marketers call that brand salience. And today, few tools build brand salience more resiliently than Martech.

At present, this overlooked aspect of your Marketing mix could lead to disproportionate gains for those who successfully integrate Martech into their brand positioning and strategy.

Let us spare a moment dissecting this opportunity for disproportionate gains from Martech.

To do so, we will refer to the classic Customer Lifetime Value model, and pair it with the Product Adoption Life Cycle model, beginning with the Innovators.

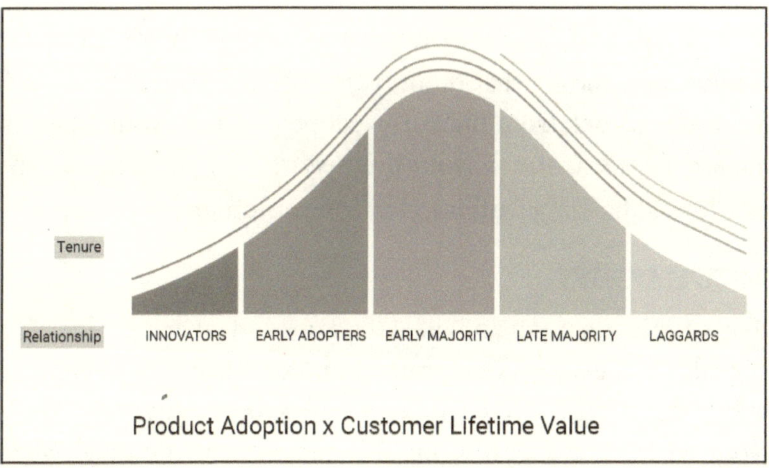

Product Adoption x Customer Lifetime Value

INNOVATORS

When you go to market, the first conversions you receive are from your Innovators. They are also the ones with the most valuable feedback. Does your Martech "go to market" the same way your brands do? One way to get an incisive answer is to ask: "Is my Martech stack designed to adapt as my product/service and market mature?"

EARLY ADOPTERS

Today's Early Adopter is tomorrow's Innovator. And, an Early Adopter in one product/service category may be an Innovator in another. Your Early Adopters are living proof that your bet with the Innovators paid off. Does your Martech have a plan for weaponising these Early Adopters into brand mascots bringing in the Early Majority?

EARLY MAJORITY

Your Early and Late Majority have different needs from the Innovators, and by that point, your offering has evolved, with critical feedback from the Early Adopters. But is your Martech poised to eke as much from this segment as possible, turning the lowest hanging fruit into lifetime customers?

LATE MAJORITY

Bad offerings sputter and die. Good ones adapt and evolve. The signals for the latter come from your Late Majority who remain while the going is good, and leave before becoming Laggards. Is your Martech stack capturing this audience before they switch to a competitor, and turning their signals into the next version of your product or service?

LAGGARDS

They say there's no party like the after party, and in some regards, that may be true for the Laggards, who are often easier to service than the more demanding Innovators or Early Adopters, but can become troublesome (think of the uninvited guest staying beyond their welcome) especially when your offering is no longer viable. Can your Martech migrate Laggards to Early Adopters of your newer offering?

The moral of the lesson is this: in taking your Martech to CX, you have to go deep (Customer LTV) as well as broad (across Adoption Curve). The easiest trick to doing this is the one we mentioned just earlier: reducing mental friction.

What *is* mental friction, and how might we apply it in going from Martech to Experience Tech?

Before we move on to our closing section, we should give sufficient scope to this question.

MENTAL FRICTION

You've already seen that reduced mental friction will make your brand top-of-mind in your customers' consideration set. This is what Marketers call TOMA, or Top-of-Mind-Awareness. But mental friction is applied equally critically in other spheres as well. Let's examine the 5 key stages of the Sales/Marketing funnel and explore Marteching™ opportunities.

Awareness

While your brand battles for TOMA, other brands are battling, too. At present, distinctive Martech tools can bring in a competitive advantage. But how sustainable is that advantage, when the market begins to adopt the same tools? You have to think creative. Sometimes, just rearranging your Martech stack could bring in that differentiation, and give you an edge you can sustain. But to keep you there, you and your team will need to go from being Martech's Early Adopters and Early Majority to being Innovators. Not only ought you to know the latest tools and trends (the things that change), but you've got to keep mapping that with perennial human and marketing truths (the things that never change).

Consideration

When a customer evaluates brands and finds you a perfect match, they aren't attributing that decision to your Martech. Or your advertising. Or your in-store experience. Of course, if you were to put them on the spot, they would feel compelled to choose one force or the other. But truth is, since a lot of this is based on intuition, they simply wouldn't know. That said, as with nature, perfection is untraceable. So let your Martech be untraceable. Any less, and it'll be visible—clunky, obtrusive, unwieldy. Work those signals that lead a prospect from awareness to consideration, and reinforce them. Notice everything, test some, and improve what you can't test. Then, watch the friction plummet. Sprinklr, a unified customer experience management (CXM) platform improves brand consideration splendidly with their proactive CX solution turning consumer insights into business opportunities at scale.

Purchase

Martech can't do everything. It isn't a magic pill. You've *got* to know the tool, AND the domain in which it is used, if you are to operate it with any distinctive competitive advantage. And here's where a certain few transaction-based tools really stand out, for reducing the friction in the buying process:

- Kount—an order processing portal that doesn't just fight chargebacks but prevents them with fraud detection rules that stay a step ahead of the most sophisticated scams;
- Adyen—a globally accepted end-to-end payments, data, and financial management platform rolled into one;
- MasterCard KAI—a chatbot that can enable your transactions, monitor spending habits and curb your spending limits, taking conversational commerce to the next level

Loyalty

What keeps customers coming back? Is it the need for a familiar experience? Is it the desire to belong in an exclusive club of like minds? Is it mere habit? Leveraging Martech in an environment where these questions aren't answered or even addressed, shows.And here, we will take a name you would never hear in a Marteching™ book: Tony Hawk. No not Stark, Hawk. Tony Hawk was a professional skater who launched a video game Pro-Skater that drove a lot of gamers towards skating. So, as far as knowing your customer went, Tony Hawk aced it; he *was* the customer. Youth bought the game, and then bought a skateboard. So far, so good. That was 1999. Fast forward 2 decades, and Tony Hawk is promoting his remastered version of the game to a generation unfamiliar with it. So how do you do the reverse? How, after creating a generation of skateboarders, do you create a generation of skate-"gamers"? The answer is always the same: by knowing your customer. Tony Hawk printed the bottom of the custom edition boards with scratch-card material, below which were hidden promo codes to in-game rewards. Sliding being one of the most common moves, skaters were bound to reveal the hidden promo code after a round of skating. Then, Tony Hawk livestreamed himself debuting the boards, and showed the scratched underside and the code. Influencers took over, and pretty soon, every skater was out there vying for these special boards, which became a privileged entry point to the gaming experience of the most talked about game launch. What can Martechers learn from this? Know your customer, know the domain, and *then* unleash Martech like nobody else would.

Advocacy

Here at last is what many Marketers consider to be the "holy grail" of their practice. Can Martech bring untold value here? Certainly. How? Well, connect the dots. If you've been reducing the mental friction in the Awareness, Consideration, Purchase and Loyalty phases, you've reduced the changes of not being recommended when the time comes. If your brand keeps a relatively high Net Promoter Score, you may wish to consider:

- Influitive: gamified customer advocacy
- Ambassador: transparent referral engine
- Firstup: insight-based employee championing
- Call Miner: customer feedback management

And with that, we close another section, and move on to the final, where we will look at the promise and peril of a Marteching™ future.

~ ~ ~ ~

PART IV

LIFE

Chapter 14

The Promise, the Peril, the Future

When a couple come together in holy matrimony, they pledge to remain together during good times and bad, sickness and health, for rich or for poor, until death do them part.

As we will see, that pledge has a lot to do with the coming together of Marketing and Technology in the form of the singular entity we call Marteching™.

The Promise: "Good Times..."

This entire book contains the promise of Marteching™. While it has highlighted the revolutionary changes underway in Martech, it has also given due credence to fundamentals which never change: to Marketing.

So what changes, and what remains? Well, that's for you, the Martecher, to deliver on. This book serves as a guidepost and sounding board, but this is your show.

That said, we do wish to feature one last element hitherto unseen by you in this book, and that is, a demonstration of the promise of Marteching™ with a live collaboration.

We decided to unleash ChatGPT, and gave it a few instructions:

1. Present a 150-word summary of AI transforming Marketing, with case studies
2. Break that down into iambic pentameter
3. Write a plot summary on the same theme for an Indiana Jones sequel set in Wakanda
4. Deliver an Oscars acceptance speech, but have the orchestra cut it off

Here is the result.

This Section was Written by ChatGPT

Headline: The Transformative Power of AI in Martech: Revolutionizing the Marketing Landscape

Summary:

Artificial Intelligence (AI) has emerged as a game-changer in the marketing industry, revolutionizing the way businesses approach marketing technology (Martech). With the advent of Assistive AI and Generative AI, among other AI applications, marketers now have access to powerful tools that enhance their decision-making, campaign optimization, and customer experiences.

Assistive AI provides marketers with intelligent insights and predictive analytics, enabling data-driven strategies and personalized customer targeting. It empowers marketers to make informed decisions and streamline their campaigns for maximum impact. Generative AI, on the other hand, unlocks unparalleled creativity by producing compelling content, such as personalized ads, social media posts, and even video campaigns.

Case studies:

- Personalization at Scale: Coca-Cola leveraged AI-powered Assistive AI platforms to analyze customer data and deliver personalized marketing messages. By understanding individual preferences and purchase patterns, Coca-Cola achieved a significant uplift in engagement and conversions, leading to improved brand loyalty.

- Content Creation Reinvented: Airbnb utilized Generative AI to automatically generate localized travel recommendations and personalized content for their users. This approach allowed Airbnb to deliver highly relevant and engaging content at scale, enhancing user experiences and driving increased bookings.
- Enhanced Customer Support: Nike employed AI-powered chatbots to provide real-time assistance and personalized recommendations to customers. Through natural language processing and machine learning, Nike's chatbots improved response times, resolved queries efficiently, and gathered valuable customer insights for future marketing strategies.
- Predictive Analytics for Campaign Optimization: Amazon harnessed AI-driven predictive analytics to optimize their marketing campaigns. By analyzing vast amounts of customer data, Amazon identified patterns and preferences, enabling them to target the right customers with the right offers, resulting in improved conversion rates and sales growth.

As AI continues to advance, the marketing industry is witnessing a transformational shift. With Assistive AI and Generative AI as valuable tools, marketers are empowered to make data-driven decisions, personalize customer experiences, create compelling content, and optimize campaigns. AI's impact on

Martech is undeniable, reshaping the marketing landscape and enabling businesses to thrive in an increasingly competitive digital world.

★ ★ ★

Artificial Intelligence reshapes Martech's field,
With Assistive AI and Generative might revealed.
Marketers harness these tools to redefine,
Their strategies, guided by AI's design.

Assistive AI provides insights, wise and sound,
Predictive analytics, decisions profound.
Marketers leverage data to drive success,
With AI's assistance, they truly impress.

Generative AI fuels creative inspiration,
Producing content that sparks fascination.
Ads, posts, and videos, a captivating sight,
AI's artistic prowess shining bright.

Let's explore recent case studies in this domain,
Where AI's impact has left an indelible stain.
Coca-Cola's personalized approach took flight,
Thanks to AI, their engagement reached new heights.

Airbnb utilized Generative AI's immense power,
Creating tailored recommendations by the hour.
Personalized content led to increased bookings,
AI's contribution truly worth the accolades it tookings.

Nike employed AI-powered chatbots with finesse,
Enhancing customer support, their success did impress.
Real-time assistance and recommendations so bright,
AI's prowess improved Nike's customer delight.

Amazon's use of predictive analytics, a sight to behold,
Fine-tuning marketing campaigns, a story of bold.
AI's insights targeted the right customers with precision,
Driving conversions and growth, a marketing decision.

In conclusion, AI's influence on Martech is clear,
With Assistive and Generative AI steering the sphere.
Marketers embrace the power AI brings,
Innovating strategies and soaring on AI's wings.

As AI continues to evolve and expand,
Marketers must grasp its capabilities firsthand.
With AI as a partner, success they shall find,
In this poetic shift, where Martech is redefined.

★ ★ ★

Title: Indiana Jones and the Wakandan Brand Nexus: Unleashing Marketing Technology

Plot Summary: Renowned archaeologist Indiana Jones embarks on an exhilarating sequel set in the hidden nation of Wakanda. Driven by his insatiable thirst for adventure and discovery, Indy finds himself on a quest where the treasure is the elusive concept of brand growth. Armed with the powerful weaponry of data and accompanied by his brilliant AI sidekick, Byte, Indy navigates the intricate landscape of cross-cultural collaboration, symbolizing the harmonious union of marketing and technology—Martech.

(Act 1) Indiana Jones receives a cryptic message that leads him to Wakanda, a technologically advanced nation with deep-rooted traditions. Recognizing the untapped potential of combining marketing and technology, Indy partners with Wakandan marketing experts, forging a unique alliance between ancient wisdom and cutting-edge innovation. Together, they set out to unlock the secrets of brand growth within the enigmatic borders of Wakanda.

(Act 2) Immersed in the rich tapestry of Wakandan culture, Indiana Jones delves into the vast repositories of data-driven insights. Guided by Byte, an advanced AI sidekick, Indy discovers the transformative power of leveraging data as a weapon to forge powerful marketing strategies. Through collaborative efforts and cross-cultural exchanges, the boundaries between marketing and technology blur, unveiling new possibilities for brand growth.

(Bridge) Resistance emerges from traditionalists who fear the integration of marketing and technology. Indy's team must overcome skepticism, showcasing real-world examples of successful Martech collaborations. As they break down barriers, the alliance between ancient traditions and modern technology becomes a metaphor for the synergistic power of marketing and technology working hand-in-hand.

(Act 3) In a thrilling climax, Indiana Jones confronts a formidable adversary—a skeptical industry titan who clings to outdated marketing practices. Armed with the arsenal of data-driven insights and AI-powered strategies, Indy dismantles their arguments, revealing the undeniable strength of the Martech alliance. Through cross-cultural collaboration, they demonstrate how brand growth can be achieved by embracing the transformative power of marketing technology.

(Resolution) As the adventure concludes, Indiana Jones and his Wakandan allies stand as champions of cross-cultural collaboration between marketing and technology. Their journey serves as a rallying cry for the industry to embrace the Martech revolution and harness the potential of data and AI for unprecedented brand growth. The story becomes a testament to the importance of uniting ancient wisdom and technological innovation to create a brighter future for businesses worldwide.

(Ending) Indiana Jones and the Wakandan Brand Nexus celebrates the power of cross-cultural collaboration, where marketing and technology converge to unlock remarkable brand growth opportunities. Set against the backdrop of Wakanda's awe-inspiring landscapes, this thrilling sequel inspires marketers to embrace the Martech revolution. Together, we embark on a new era, where the harmonious integration of marketing and technology becomes the catalyst for extraordinary brand success.

★ ★ ★

"Ladies and gentlemen, esteemed guests, I am truly humbled and grateful for this remarkable recognition of our film,

Indiana Jones and the Wakandan Brand Nexus. It has been an incredible journey, and I want to thank the amazing cast and crew who poured their hearts into this project. I am especially grateful to the Academy for acknowledging the importance of data-driven marketing and its impact on brand growth. This award is a testament to the power of technological innovation in our industry. To the brilliant actors, led by the incomparable Harrison Ford, your performances brought these characters to life and captivated audiences worldwide. And let's not forget our AI sidekick, a virtual companion who added humor and intelligence to our story. Our director, writers, and the entire production team deserve heartfelt appreciation for their dedication and vision. The visual effects and production designers transported us to the stunning landscapes of Wakanda, making the experience truly unforgettable. To our audiences, your unwavering support fuels our passion for storytelling. Thank you for embracing the spirit of adventure that Indiana Jones embodies."

[Orchestra begins playing]

"Ah, it seems our time has been cut short. Thank you all for this tremendous honor. This award is a testament to the power of embracing innovation in our industry."

[Applause as the speech is cut off]

...and we're back.

Quite promising, wouldn't you think? And to think Digital Media agencies are still stuck in Adtechland, while Martechers have all the fun...

The Peril: "…and Bad Times…"

No discourse on tech-enabled Marketing could ever be possible without highlighting some of the perils, key among them being cybersecurity, which we will come to in a minute.

The Threat of Complexity

Every Martecher is called to tame the Martech beast. It is complex, can be unwieldy, and could unleash more harm than good in the wrong hands. (Think of a chainsaw in the hands of a woodcutter who's had zero lumberjack training.) This is where books, tutorials, conferences and other learning aids can greatly aid marketers in navigating and dominating this new field.

The Threat of Knavery

The Ad Fraud Squad never sleep. They single handedly give Adtech a bad rep, and yet, nobody wants to talk about it. But for all their schemes, be it ad stacking, page refreshing, duplicated bid requests (causing advertisers to bid against themselves), or whatever next, you can narrow ad fraud down to two specialty areas: click fraud and impression fraud. While the scope of the dupery can make the head swim, we'd recommend looking up Dr. Augustine Fou, who has been quietly covering this unreported segment for well over 2 decades now. He'll quietly keep you ahead of the scammers.

The Threat to Privacy

As with any new relationship, transparency and trust are critical. How personal can you get when you're in a relationship? How far is too far? It is the same with Martech. We are dealing with personal data of customers, vendors, employees and other stakeholders which must be protected at all costs. One breach of trust is all it takes for everything to fall apart, and rebuilding can be a lot harder than building from scratch.

The Threat to Security

While a threat to privacy may affect individuals, a threat to security can affect the entire system. And since Data Governance is a matter of compliance, you've got to leave no stone unturned in ensuring a robust Martech stack that meets or exceeds the requirements. A company that is clueless about where its data lives, how it is accessed and by whom, only increases its own risk and eventual operational complexity, when things go south. Look into one-stop cybersecurity solutions like Cyral or Illumio: open-source data cloud services operating on a zero-trust architecture. You can't be too careful.

The Threat of Knowing-it-All

The more you know, the less you know. That's just one of the maxims of life: there's always going to be more where that came from, particularly in a field as dynamic as Martech. We could give you the names of a few Martechers at the top of their game, but we'll just give you two: Scott Brinker and Franz Riemersma. You find these two, you'll find the lot, because they operate at the junction where Marteching™ meets. A particularly helpful resource is their annual award show Stackie, which showcases some of the most well-"stacked" Martech environments. Every 5 minutes spent learning from smart Martechers like these are equal to about 30 research hours. If you don't believe us, head on over to YouTube and search for "Martech 2023 Big Picture", and you'll see what we mean.

The Future: "...Until Death do us Part."

A relationship is as rich as you make it. So what *is* the Marteching™ relationship cut out for? What are the limits of possibility here? Before we bring this book to a close, we'd like to answer that question.

And since we are Marketers first, and technologists second, you will hear the future of Marteching™ from a Marketer's perspective. Are you ready? Because we're itching to shoot.

What IS Marketing? The stimulus for a give and take between buyer and seller. When the seller provides the stimulus, the buyer responds with patronage. When the buyer provides the stimulus, the seller responds with an offering. You see, Marketing works both ways. Know who gets this better than most? Data. Data is present at every imaginable end point, bringing marketing touchpoints from the dark, so to say, into the light. Once they're in the light, the journey has only just begun. What will you do with this data? What does it mean? What sort of data constellation would best illuminate the way forward? But data is only the fuel. What's the engine? Martech. And, it takes an engineering mind to truly grasp the marvel of it. Those who do will not just respond, but be a part of the stimulus. Their perspective of Martech will add every bit—if not more—to Marteching™ than a new Martech tool, service or platform might. Where do these perspectives come from? 2 places: observation and reflection. A Martecher that observes and reflects will write the future of this business. And, they'll be the ones in the drivers' seat. (See why we featured a DeLorean on the cover?) Ours isn't a business of bits and bytes. Ours is a business of synapses and neurons, of sinew and tendon, of headlines and heartbeats and adrenaline shots administered via 60-second commercial. Lose this, and you may as well stop calling it Martech. Because when you see the complete picture, you can never unsee it. Just like Total

Football. And that is why, you will never unlock Martech value so long as you see things in silos. Yes, we need them strategically, but not as much operationally. Once you're able to take in the "Total" perspective, you will begin to be fed by insights and trends from areas far beyond your core skill. And that will enrich your practice. The more enriched a Martecher, the more it enriches Marteching™. And that is why, one of the first case studies we introduced in this book was the Mill BLACKBIRD®: the world's first fully adjustable car rig that creates photoreal CG. Is that Martech? If yes, where does it fit in the Martech stack? If we limited ourselves to just those tools which can fit inside a tech stack, this book would've been as thin as a blog post. Or the Dominos Knock Box, an idea that predates Google Maps. What could we learn from that? Well if you remember that one, it was about the magic that can happen when you ask an industrial designer to solve a communication problem. You end up in a very different place than you might expect, and the process is anything but linear. As we work towards building the Marteching™ industry together, let us not leave behind what made the brands we work on famous. What made some of them endure decades, even centuries? If the Marteching™ rebrand of Marketing is to be a successful, it will require every one of our perspectives. So bring it. If you're a 40-yr old marketer learning code, bring it. If you're a 20-yr old design student unsure how your fine arts degree can aid Marteching™, bring it. If you're a data analyst seeking to add value in how brand stories are told, bring it. If you're a CMO considering a marketing memoir that tells all, bring it. If you're a burned out Martecher looking forward to taking a sabbatical from it all, bring it.

See you out there.

~ ~ ~ ~

www.ingramcontent.com/pod-product-compliance
Lightning Source LLC
LaVergne TN
LVHW041207150826
845673LV00001B/323

* 9 7 9 8 8 9 0 6 6 8 7 3 8 *